ROUTLEDGE LIBRARY EDITIONS:
SOUTH AFRICA

Volume 6

SOUTH AFRICA'S RULE
OF VIOLENCE

SOUTH AFRICA'S RULE
OF VIOLENCE

PATRICK DUNCAN

Routledge
Taylor & Francis Group

LONDON AND NEW YORK

First published in 1964 by Methuen & Co Ltd.

This edition first published in 2023
by Routledge
4 Park Square, Milton Park, Abingdon, Oxon OX14 4RN

and by Routledge
605 Third Avenue, New York, NY 10158

Routledge is an imprint of the Taylor & Francis Group, an informa business

British Library Cataloguing in Publication Data
A catalogue record for this book is available from the British Library

ISBN: 978-1-032-30347-5 (Set)
ISBN: 978-1-032-33359-5 (Volume 6) (hbk)
ISBN: 978-1-032-33363-2 (Volume 6) (pbk)
ISBN: 978-1-003-31933-7 (Volume 6) (ebk)

DOI: 10.4324/9781003319337

Publisher's Note
The publisher has gone to great lengths to ensure the quality of this reprint but points out that some imperfections in the original copies may be apparent.

Disclaimer
The publisher has made every effort to trace copyright holders and would welcome correspondence from those they have been unable to trace.

This is a reissue of a previously published book. The language is reflective of the time in which this book was published. In reissuing this book, no offence is intended by the Publishers to any reader.

SOUTH AFRICA'S
RULE OF VIOLENCE

Patrick Duncan

METHUEN & CO LIMITED
11 NEW FETTER LANE · LONDON EC4

First published in 1964
© 1964 *Patrick Duncan*
Printed in Great Britain by
T. H. Brickell & Son Ltd
Gillingham, Dorset

Contents

Abbreviations

A	*The Cape Argus*, Cape Town, daily
B	*Die Burger*, Cape Town, daily
C	*Contact*, Cape Town, fortnightly
CT	*Cape Times*, Cape Town, daily
D	*Dagbreek*, Johannesburg, weekly
DD	*Daily Dispatch*, East London, daily
F	*The Friend*, Bloemfontein, daily
FT	*Fighting Talk* (suppressed), Johannesburg, monthly
G	*The Guardian*, Manchester, daily
N	*New Statesman*, London, weekly
NA	*New Age* (suppressed), Cape Town, weekly
O	*The Observer*, London, weekly
P	*Golden City Post*, Johannesburg, weekly
PN	*Pretoria News*, Pretoria, daily
RDM	*Rand Daily Mail*, Johannesburg, daily
S	*The Star*, Johannesburg, daily
SE	*Sunday Express*, Johannesburg, weekly
ST	*Sunday Times*, Johannesburg, weekly
W	*The World*, Johannesburg, weekly
WS	*Weekly Star* (*Tabloid*)
X	*The Africa X-Ray Report*, Johannesburg (ceased publication)

Indented passages are uncredited quotations from original sources.

Foreword

This book describes some of the bitter fruits of the apartheid system, the South African government's official doctrine of race separation and domination.

It describes a series of assaults, cruelties, reckless brutalities and atrocities unparalleled since the death of Hitler. It describes them carefully and documents them. It is the story of how the flesh and bones of powerless people have been torn, crushed, burnt, and electrically shocked by the supporters of apartheid.

This book therefore bypasses the now familiar debate between the supporters and the enemies of the South African government, as to whether in this moment of history, 'development' should be 'separate' or not.

Such words are vague and abstract. Even the word 'apartheid' has never been properly defined.

The thesis of this book is that any system that can produce cruelties on this scale must be a bad system. Whether ideologists are or are not able to make their case for 'separation' is quite irrelevant.

The thesis of this book is that the cruelties are so bad that every decent member of the human race must help those who are trying to stop them. An end must be made to apartheid.

Many commentators have of recent months, as if in a set formula, expressed their 'abhorrence' of apartheid. But in the same breath they have argued against practical steps to end apartheid. If they will read these true accounts of what it feels like to be black and to be ruled by apartheid, perhaps they will be less ready to let empty expressions of disapproval slip from their lips. Perhaps they will understand that the apartheid issue is one of the great watersheds of history.

There have been, perhaps, four political issues of supreme

9

importance during our century: the Russian revolution, the Spanish civil war, the second world war, and the clash of colour. It is possible that of all these the last-named will turn out to have been the greatest. For where the Russian revolution and the Spanish clash stirred tens of millions, and the second world war stirred hundreds of millions, the clash of colour looks like stirring billions.

And it should never be forgotten that to the leaders of these billions the apartheid issue, however small an area it may occupy, and however few people are involved, is already a symbol of the world-wide clash of colour.

The characteristic of these great world issues is that they present the leaders of mankind with the need to make decisions in an unusual, somewhat unfamiliar dimension: the dimension of right and wrong. For in normal-sized questions they can always decide on what will pay best, make a small bow in the direction of morality, and jog along in their chosen direction. But when a Hitler arises these commercial criteria are not enough. Stark choices are presented to statesmen, and, as Neville Chamberlain discovered, woe betide those too blind to see that the commercial dimension is then no longer enough.

An issue now faces the great countries of Europe and America no less important than the issue of nazism. Like nazism it concerns a doctrine about the nature of man. As at the time of nazism, too, wrong decisions, decisions made for commercial reasons, can lead the human race into the depths.

In the thirties and forties men arose who were able to see the implications of nazism. Men arose with the vision to lift the whole question out of the ordinary rut, and up to the other dimension of right and wrong. Is it possible to hope that now, in the sixties, men will arise who are once again equal to the times, who are able to look at this new issue, to consider the implications of the racist view in 1964, to see fearlessly what racism in fact does to people in South Africa, and to make right decisions, however immediately unprofitable or unpopular they may be?

I think the answer is Yes. At any rate I challenge anyone, whether he be a leader or not, to read this book carefully and then to deny that the problem of apartheid does indeed lie in the moral dimension.

And if the problem does lie in the moral dimension, then it follows that a duty lies on all who have the power to use their power against evil and for good.

Some things need to be said before the book is read. The first concerns my attitude to the Afrikaner people. It is a fact that the non-white people hate the Afrikaner people, and that they do not hate the other white South Africans so much. A recent public opinion poll of the Institute of Race Relations shows that this is true of Africans. Probably further research would show that it is true of the coloured people and the people of Indian origin too. This book shows that this hatred is based on fact, for nearly all these cases of cruelty concern Afrikaner, not English, South Africans. I believe that although the whites as a whole are not guiltless, yet the Afrikaners carry a heavier load of guilt. Having said this I want readers to know that I selected telling cases of apartheid-inspired cruelty, irrespective of whether the perpetrators were white or non-white, Afrikaner or English.

To the best of my knowledge all the records used in this book are true. But I must enter several cautions. They are mostly based on press reports. To have collected copies of court records and affidavits would have been beyond my powers and resources. But court records are public documents. According to the magistrates' court act a court *must* give any member of the public a copy of the records of that court. And I accordingly commend as a project the collection of the records of the cases referred to in this book. Surely there is some institute, some foundation, somewhere, that is concerned enough with this problem, the problem of the violence behind racism, to investigate the whole question impartially and to document it.

Over fifteen years (for I have collected records since 1948) I have inevitably missed many cases. During those years I did a good deal of travelling, and several times broke the sequence of following the newspapers. I spent a year in Britain in 1949 and 1950. And in 1962 and the early part of 1963 I was living in the mountains of southern Basutoland in so isolated a place that I could not get a daily newspaper. (The post for my village and the surrounding villages was carried by a runner and I could not burden him with the bulk and weight of a South African daily.)

Again, it must constantly be remembered that the press only reported a small percentage of the cases in which policemen were prosecuted. And only a very small percentage of the atrocities committed by the police ever come to court. Police violence and torture against the oppressed is commonplace; it is accepted as a necessary tool of repression. And so prosecutions are initiated by only a few commanding officers. Violence against prisoners in cells is easy to conceal. And a single complainant's word cannot prevail against a denial, even if the denial is uncorroborated, for a prosecution to succeed. This book, thus, is in the nature of an understatement, for many of the worst excesses remain almost certainly uninvestigated and unreported.

Another caution: many of the cases were inadequately reported. Sometimes evidence was headlined, while judgments were either tucked away in a subsequent issue or unreported. Let me hasten however to pay a tribute to the much-criticized

'English press' of South Africa. No daily paper exists in South Africa that speaks up for democracy for all. But many true democrats work on these papers. And, over many years, these democrats have used the sub-editor's glue and scissors, or the reporter's sharp pencil, to castigate the crimes of apartheid, and to defend democracy by implication.

Where, in these terrible tales of cruelty, I have recorded evidence, but omitted reference to court judgments, the responsibility is often mine. The reason is that it was not my aim to chronicle the failures or successes of the judicial system, but merely to preserve the memory of the peculiar manifestations of apartheid-inspired cruelty.

It may be objected that the book is one-sided: 'You have reported wrongs done by white to non-white: you have been silent about wrongs done by non-white to white.' My reason is simple: my sole purpose is to record the peculiar form that violence takes when it is used in support of a racialist state. Of course, violence is found everywhere. Of course, whites *are* wronged in South Africa. But such violence does not form part of the pattern of apartheid-inspired violence, and thus does not find a place in this book.

My thesis is that a special form of cruelty is produced when one group which is powerless is handed over into the power of another group, and when hostility exists between the two groups. This special form of cruelty cannot for obvious reasons be committed by Africans in South Africa against whites. (What is done by Africans in Bechuanaland against the semi-slave pigmy Masarwa people is another question which can be noted here, but, for reasons already given, cannot be dealt with in this book.)

My thesis is that apartheid breeds cruelty of a reckless, revolting, and special kind; that the special atmosphere of the

13

reports of these acts of cruelty is the authentic smell of life in South Africa; and that, in view of the mounting importance of the apartheid issue, the world should know and be able to recognize this smell.

CHAPTER ONE
What is Apartheid?

According to the South Africa Act of 1909 (an act of the British parliament, and also the constitution of South Africa) political power in South Africa is limited to whites. No non-white may vote for, or be elected to, parliament or any of the provincial councils.* The nature of society in South Africa agrees with this constitution, and the three million whites have taken for themselves all power and the right to enjoy nearly all the good things of life. The thirteen million Africans, coloured people, and people of Indian origin have been turned into second-class citizens in their own country, without votes, without the right to own land, excluded by law from good jobs, kept poor by law and custom, despised and oppressed.

No one had ever heard of apartheid before about 1946. A general election for the whites-only parliament was due to be held in 1948. The vaguely pro-British, vaguely democratic, government of General Jan Christian Smuts was expected to be re-elected. The nationalist party of Dr Malan, hostile to Africans, and at that time openly hostile to Jews too, invented the word '*apartheid*' to try to get floating white voters to vote against Smuts. In parliament the nationalists had one main cry: that Smuts loved the British too much and that he did too much for 'the natives'. The nationalists tried, in the event with success, to frighten the white voters with a fear of the Africans. Smuts, they alleged, could not defend them from the Africans. The nationalists alone knew how to keep the non-whites in their place. '*Die kaffer op sy plek: die koelie uit die land*', (the kaffir

*The vestigial 'coloured vote' in the Cape Province, and the fraudulent 'independence' of the Transkei with its adult suffrage deserve, but only just deserve, mention in this footnote: both are worthless.

– an insulting word for African – in his place, and the coolie – an insulting word for persons of Indian and Pakistani origin – out of the country), such was their election cry. And this policy of toughness to the non-whites they called '*apartheid*', meaning apartness, separation. It was supposed to be a shining new policy that would 'solve the native problem'.

It is now a word that is known round the world. Often it is pronounced wrong. The correct pronunciation is not 'appetite', not 'apathite', not 'apart-hite'. The correct pronunciation is 'apart-hate'.

It is a word that is probably destined to mobilize the world against this latter-day nazism, this new rule of the *herrenvolk*. It is a word that put the nationalists into power in 1948 and that is probably destined to put the whites out of power in the nineteen-sixties.

What is apartheid? As we have seen, in 1948, it was an election cry which was never clearly defined. Between 1948 and 1964 the authorities introduced a good many changes and innovations sharpening and brutalizing South Africa's traditional white supremacy and segregation.

They removed what they called 'black spots' – i.e. groups of non-whites living on land of their own which was surrounded by white-owned land. Since white-owned land is nearly always inhabited by more non-whites than whites the 'removal of black spots' nearly always means the 'removal of black freedom'. Because blacks remain, but as serfs, servants and squatters. We will look at the condition of agricultural serfs and squatters in Chapter 12.

They removed Sophiatown, Johannesburg, and many other urban townships. These townships were creating the serious offence of allowing relatively free Africans to live near white suburbs. Many of these townships, like Sophiatown, were much older than their white neighbours which had surrounded them in an urban sprawl. Prior occupancy, however, means little to white South Africa. With a little bit of propaganda prior occupancy can even be turned into 'unhistory'. This has happened in the case of occupation of the whole country. It is safe to say that on April 6, 1652, when the Dutch colonization began, there was not one magisterial district (as now defined) which was empty of people. Khoi-Khoin graziers watched the whites landing on the beaches of Table Bay. Yet, today, paid propagandists have persuaded thousands of Europeans and Americans that the whites actually got to South Africa before the non-whites.

Under the apartheid system from 1948 onwards the authorities multiplied the outward and visible signs of segregation and intensified the petty humiliations of it.

It was as if a Moloch needed to force each citizen, at some point in each day's course, to bow in his direction. Many people use railways stations, so these were a favourite place for enforcing Moloch-worship. The large entrances would be allocated to the various 'races'. Sometimes, as at Cape Town, the segregatory notices would be three feet high and twenty feet long. Mingling on the street the 'races' would be compelled, under the eye of the railway police, to pass through the entrance allocated to each 'race'. But these separate entrances led to the same concourse, where, once again, the 'races' would mingle.

The authorities extricated the Africans from the body politic in every imaginable way. Where education for all had been directed by the Departments of Education, that for Africans was, in future, to be a subdivision of Bantu Affairs. Where the Department of Social Welfare had controlled, let us say, all schools for handicapped children, under Verwoerd's vigilance, reminiscent of Deuteronomy, those for handicapped African children were placed under the Bantu Administration and Development Department.

In at least one case, that of unemployment insurance, the change involved the theft of millions of pounds, the compulsory contributions of African employees. These were easily dealt with: most African contributors had their right to draw benefits abolished, and their contributions were transferred to general revenue.

One of the major problems facing the authorities was the fact that no one had even satisfactorily defined the racial categories. Human beings are so different and so varied that the words 'native', 'European', 'coloured', 'Indian' could not easily be applied to all. There were always anomalies.

This problem has been tackled with energy. Expense has not been spared. A vast building was built at Pretoria to carry records of the genetic inheritance of every single human being in the country. Borderline cases were summoned into local headquarters of the Population Registration Department. Pencils were pushed into people's hair, to judge whether the crimp exceeded the maximum permitted degree for 'Europeans'. Angles of noses were taken. Clothes were removed for the tints of unexposed skin to be assessed. Relations, long since dead, were discussed, to determine whether the family was 'coloured' or not.

In one notorious case a school child of 16 committed suicide when his family was 'demoted' to a lower racial group. For 'demotion' would mean removal to a new suburb, loss of job, and disappearance of most friends and relatives.

Nearly always did the authorities see to it that in these demarcations, removals, and divisions, the whites came off best. For the authorities had been voted into power by the whites – and the ticket had been apartheid.

In the fifteen years since the nationalists won the 1948 election, their apartheid policy has become totalitarian. That is to say, it now seeks to impose its doctrine on every part of human life, however private, and however sacred. In practice, apartheid blunts and corrupts some of the finest instincts in man. For instance, most people feel an instinct of love and protectiveness towards babies, even other peoples' babies, even the babies of national or tribal enemies. This normal instinct is blunted or suppressed by apartheid. In 1961 a white girl refused water for a hungry nine-months-old baby. The reason was that the baby was of Indian origin, and the girl lived in the Orange Free State, a province that prides itself on being 'koelievry' (free of coolies). The father was travelling through in a car when it happened. He told the press: We reached Brandfort, and the baby started crying. We needed hot water to make milk, so I went to a café. Over the door was a 'Europeans Only' sign but I explained to a white girl and asked if she could help. She replied curtly 'No water'. (A 29/8/61)

The normal instinct to educate children to love others is perverted. In Tzaneen, Transvaal, a headmaster taught racehate to the pupils of his school whom he assembled to watch him burn a blazer of that school ceremoniously. The blazer had been worn by an African boy, and therefore, according to the beliefs of white supremacy, had been ritually soiled. (ST 1961)

The instinct to teach is blunted. Charitable whites near Vereeniging began to build a school for African children. But other whites protested that the school was too near to white smallholders. The government ordered the builders to stop, after they had spent £500 on building material and given months of their time to the project. (SE 12/10/58)

After thirty years of teaching, the St James's Catholic school for African children at Magaliesburg, Transvaal, was ordered not to reopen. The written order was received on the day the school was due to reopen in January 1957. It, too, was felt to be 'too close' to white farmers. (CT 23/1/57.) Many other great schools have also been destroyed.

The home-building instinct is destroyed. Instances of the senseless moving of people are so many as to be impossible to quote, or even to tabulate. Fifteen hundred people were suddenly driven from their homes on the farm Onverwacht in the Weenen district of Natal, on May 4, 1958. Days later a thousand of them were hiding in the bush. They had not even had time to pack. Over a period of three days the police pounced on them from early dawn and gave them marching orders. Armed with rifles and revolvers, assegais and batons, the police set fire to the grass huts, and used bulldozers to push down all other types of houses. Some of the people were taken to court. (P 4/5/58)

And under the Group Areas Act, which empowers government to move people around for racial reasons, homes are destroyed and the right to property subverted. Often people lose all their savings through forced sales under this act. The authorities expelled Hinderjeet Maharaj from his four-bedroomed house in Percy Osborn Road, Durban, and sold the house, worth £2,500, for £10. The government was the buyer. It is true that under the Act more will have to be given to Mr Maharaj, but not nearly the full value of the house. In this way the home-building instinct is discouraged and destroyed. (A 4/11/61)

Home itself is legislated out of existence for some. 'Our laws are such that literally thousands have no right to live anywhere, or no knowledge of where they have a right to live and how to get there', said the national president of the Black Sash. (CT 1/9/61)

Even charity has been inhibited. Kent School, Massachusetts, gave a bursary of £500 and a passage to Stephen Ramasodi, a schoolboy aged 16, of St. Peter's School, Johannesburg, in 1955. The apartheid government refused him a passport, and actually claimed that the refusal was 'from the point of view of the Native youth's best interests'. (S 22/7/55.) The real reason was, of course, that apartheid frowns on Africans receiving anything better than what is received by whites, and that education abroad might make an African boy discontented with his lot when he returned.

To some, married love is possible only under a permit. An African wife may live with her husband in a town if he has established his 'qualifications'. But to do so she must be able to prove that she ordinarily and lawfully resides with him. Since African men, married and unmarried, are more and more allowed to seek work in towns only if they take accommodation in so-called 'bachelor quarters', it is often impossible for the wives to prove that they ordinarily reside with them. Nor may a wife be with her husband during the period during which he is establishing his 'qualifications'. She may then visit him for periods of up to 72 hours without permission. Special extensions of the 72 hours may be given to women who wish to conceive.

Married love is forbidden to some. An American visitor told the press that her African servant had been arrested when she went to visit her husband, who was also a servant. Commenting, Col. P. Grobler, the deputy-commissioner of police, said 'The servant should have obtained permission from the owner before going to see her husband'. (S 16/11/55)

And love, even if the relationship is permanent, is forbidden if the skins of the couple do not match in colour. An elderly couple, one a 65-year-old white man, and the other a 70-year-old coloured woman, who had been living together as man and wife, were called from their bed and arrested at 1.45 a.m.

on September 2, 1950, when a policeman saw them through their bedroom window.

One of the worst features of this case was that the court forced the aged white man to say why he had been living with the aged coloured woman. He was not able to say, proudly, that he loved her. Humiliatingly, he pleaded: 'I could not do otherwise. I was on the road and had no shelter. I met her two years ago when I was in bad circumstances. She took me in. She looked after me and bought a lorry for me to carry loads of wood'. And she said: 'When I met Willemse he was sick and poor. He did not even have a second shirt, so I looked after him'. Thus did apartheid smear her noble compassion, and force him to turn against her. (S 2/9/50)

These two were charged under the immorality act, and sentenced to three months' imprisonment. But the sentence was suspended for three years on condition the 'offence' was not repeated. It must be remembered that the offence was not extramarital intercourse, but intercourse across the colour line.

How fine that line can be appeared from the case against an Englishman and Johanna Pruin who lived together. They were acquitted after she had been made, in court, to pull up the sleeve of her dress 'so that the magistrate could examine the whiteness of her arm'.

In this case the policeman arrested the couple because 'he thought that the woman was coloured because of her high cheekbones'. (F 25/11/50)

Finally, the apartheid state has come between man and God. Although under islamic law a mosque may not be sold, exchanged, or abandoned, the South African government took over the mosques at Piet Retief and South End, Port Elizabeth because it wished to separate the races. The 'church clause' law gives the government the power to prevent Africans from attending the church of their choice. And the authorities do not hesitate to interfere with religion in the most high-handed manner, if they see fit. The police banned an ordination service on May 28, 1961 (Trinity Sunday) at St James's Mission, Cradock, Cape Province. The Bishop of Grahamstown, the Rt Rev Robert Taylor, commented: 'The ban appears to be a serious infringement of the right to worship freely'. (ST 6/5/62)

And in 1958 three deacons of the Calvin Protestant Church were fined £3 each for holding illegal church services. They were men living at Komaggas, Cape Province, a so-called coloured mission or reserve, and the prosecution was under the coloured missions and reserves act. Behind this prosecution lies a revealing story, a story of state collaboration to help the Dutch Reformed Church and to harm its competitors.

In 1949 the Calvin Protestant Church, under the headship of the Rev I. D. Morkel, broke away from the Dutch Reformed Church because that church accepted apartheid.

Most of the people at Komaggas left the D.R.C. to join the new church. Thereafter they were harassed, not only by their old church, but also by the government. A regulation was finally passed in October 1957 which had the effect of making all church services except Dutch Reformed services illegal. Thereafter church services were taken by deacons of the Calvin church. They were prosecuted and sentenced, and their application to appeal was refused.

The reaction of their flocks was to join in silent prayer, not to try to re-unite with the D.R.C. (*Daily News* 6/3/58; NA 20/3/58)

Like other totalitarian states, the apartheid state has shown that in its view there is no corner of life that is free from government interference.

And in the same way as in other totalitarian states, life itself resists the overweening claims of the state. And therefore, in many respects, the state becomes anti-life. And, as we have

23

seen, this hostility to life is manifested in violence. Sometimes the violence is private, and sometimes it is public, inflicted by organs of the state.

Let us first look at violence by organs of the state, and by persons such as the police and the prison warders, who are placed by the state in positions in which violence is possible and easy to commit against the powerless non-whites in their control.

Then it will be appropriate to look at violence on the farms. South Africa's farms are so organized that a tremendous amount of power is held by the white farmers, and hardly any by the non-white labourers. This situation, too, is fertile in breeding violence. Having looked at concrete cases of violence in the name of white supremacy on the farms, it will be appropriate to look at some of the legal and social framework which allows these things to happen.

Lastly a short look will be taken at violence by ordinary white people, not police and not farmers, against non-whites, in maintenance (as some whites see it) of the white supremacy system of apartheid.

CHAPTER TWO

The Reputation of the Police

Our age, the heir of the age of Hitler and Stalin, has had its fill of stories of violence and horror. We are therefore constantly tempted to shrug our shoulders when we learn of new atrocities, and to say to ourselves that they are either too far away, or involve people too different from ourselves, for it to matter much.

We must resist such a temptation, for compassion is not expendable. All know in our hearts that the world is one, and that what is suffered today by our brother on the other side of the world with our connivance, is partly our responsibility. And, in addition, it may well be suffered by us tomorrow.

And so it was well done when *The Observer*, one of the small group of the world's greatest newspapers and a noble champion, over many years, of justice, published in November 1963 the story of how eleven detainees, just released from Pretoria Central prison, had been tortured while they were in prison. Their stories were told in sworn statements. Here are excerpts from the account:

> Three of the 11 give details of torture by electric shock methods which were first used in Algeria.
>
> The names of the detainees and of the policemen they mention in their affidavits have been withheld to protect them, as they are still in South Africa.
>
> B was arrested in Cape Town last June, and was transferred to Pretoria in August. 'On arrival I was called into an office where I found Lieutenant S, who asked me some questions which I was unable to answer. Then S said he had no time to waste, I should be taken away and shock my brains into remembering. . . .
>
> 'They immediately took me to another office, where Ser-

geant G and another ordered me to undress myself. I was left with only my underpants. They started to hit me while undressing with clenched fists. For some days I could not open my jaw. They handcuffed me and ordered me to squat with my knees protruding above my arms which were handcuffed so that I was placed in a helpless position.

'A canvas bag was pulled over my head to the neck, which made breathing very difficult. . . . I could feel something tied round my two thumbs and my left little finger. From there I felt the electric shock as if it were being switched on and off time and again. At the same time they kept on asking me questions as they switched off, and when I refused to answer the questions they switched on.

'At one stage I felt a blow on the right side under my armpit as if it was a kick. They did this to me until I promised I would answer the questions, and then they removed the handcuffs and the canvas bag. I was ordered to dress.'

P was also arrested last June while trying to get to Bechuanaland. He was taken to Pretoria in July. 'When I came in there were several of the Special Branch men including Mr F [whose name is mentioned by several of the detainees].

'I was choked and my neck ringed up and twisted. They all started hitting me with fists and kicked me about. At this stage Mr F was sitting behind the desk.

'A canvas bag was put over my head. . . . Then I felt something like wire tied to my little fingers on both hands. Then I felt electric shocks which were applied occasionally. Then I would be lifted up by the stick and be left to drop down on my back. . . .

'All the time they were doing this to me they were forcing me to admit that I know Mr G [one of the accused in the sabotage trial] and Mr Sachs [Albie Sachs, a Cape Town barrister now held under the 90-days detention law]. . . . I was whipped with a hosepipe and also judo chops [were] applied on my kidneys and on the back of my neck.

'I was handcuffed for the second time and they told me they were going to kill me and that nobody would ever ask them anything. I was put to the same treatment of electric shocks. . . . The pressure was so high that I messed myself up. Then I was released to go to the lavatory.

'On my return from the lavatory the same treatment was applied and I messed myself up again.'

Two of the detainees tell in their affidavits what happened when they tried to report the assaults to the visiting magistrate, who, according to the Minister of Justice, Mr B. Vorster, is supposed to ensure that the detainees are properly treated.

L, a 40-year-old member of the African National Congress, says: 'I saw the visiting magistrate and reported to him that I was assaulted by the police. In reply the magistrate said "You also wanted to go to Tanganyika to learn and come back and kill the whites so they are doing what they like on you".'

This report in *The Observer* followed closely the report that a prominent Cape African member of the African National Congress, Looksmart Solwandle Ngudle, had been 'found hanged' while he was detained under the 90-day clause of the General Law Amendment Act of 1963. Strong suspicion existed that he had in fact been done to death or that he had died under torture. The facts are examined at a later stage in this book.

Reference is frequently made in this book to the '90-day clause'. This is a provision of the General Law Amendment Act of 1963. Under this provision any commissioned officer may, without warrant, arrest any person suspected of opposition activities. He may detain such person in custody for interrogation at any place he thinks fit until such person has, in the opinion of the police, answered questions put to him satisfactorily, or for ninety days, or whichever is the shorter period.

The person is to be held incommunicado. No court may order the release of a person so detained. Such person may be held for successive periods of ninety days, without any limit.

The executive has, therefore, taken power to intern people indefinitely, and the courts have lost all their power to intervene in such matters.

News reached London in November 1963 that Zeph Mothopeng, one of the top-echelon leaders of the Pan-Africanist Congress, held under this clause, had been removed to a mental hospital. I know him well. One could not wish to know anyone finer. He, if messages can still reach him, and if he can still understand them, must be assured that his friends will not rest until he is free again, and until the system that destroyed his reason has been put an end to.

In November 1963 J. Hamilton Russell, a former United Party M.P. of Cape Town, took up the question of the use of torture on 90-day detainees. He said that detainees under this clause were being tortured by the 'water treatment' (prolonged submersion in cold water), the 'gas mask treatment' and the 'electric treatment' (during which a man is tied down, sprayed with salt water, and then electrically massaged in an agonizing way). (WS 30/11/63)

The Observer report was denied officially by the commissioners of police and prisons in South Africa. And they asked that their denial be accepted on the grounds that theirs is a 'disciplined force with a reputation to uphold'. *The Observer* correctly pointed out that to say that there is discipline is not to deny torture. And *The Observer* quoted some startling facts about the South African Police: 'The last available figures show that in one year 566 officers were charged with assaults on prisoners; 311 were convicted and only 11 dismissed from the force'. (O 17/11/63)

The difference of opinion between the South African authorities and *The Observer* decided me: over many years I had been collecting material with the aim, one day, of writing a book about the brutalities by which apartheid maintains itself in power. I felt now that the day had come when this book had to be written. If the South African authorities shielded themselves behind the reputation which their police and prison authorities had built for themselves over the years, let that reputation be examined, I felt.

What do we find? In 1959 a responsible commentator could write: 'The South African Police force is the most criticized and least-popular section of the South African public service'. (X March 1959.) In 1959, also, a distinguished South African daily wrote an editorial called 'Police Emergency' quoting five facts, among others, that deserve quotation:

(1) In a series of six brothel cases it has been disclosed that a considerable number of policemen armed with public money had sexual intercourse with prostitutes 'in the line of duty'. A magistrate has called this 'shocking and reprehensible' and the Dutch Reformed Church has called it 'a violation of morality and justice'. How could these methods have been employed on this scale?

(2) Between the years 1946 and 1948, 223 policemen were charged, and 174 convicted of crimes. Between 1956 and 1958, 1,263 were charged and 840 convicted. In 1958, 2.77 per cent of the European police force of 12,000 was convicted of crime, or nearly three policemen out of every 100.

(3) A detective sergeant giving evidence under oath said: 'It is an everyday occurrence for prisoners to be beaten by the police . . . usually a garden hose but sometimes a stick . . . if I hit an African over the head with the kierie it would cut open his head and injure his skull, but a hose will not

29

do that.' In sketching this background to police work, was this man perjuring himself?

(4) In May, 1959, the Commissioner of Police 'issued instructions' to the Force warning policemen not to ill-treat prisoners: 'Instructions have been telexed to every man-jack. I have instructed them that in every case that comes to notice there should be an inquiry.' The Minister of Justice said that he had 'often' given this warning. What was the situation which required these special instructions?

(5) A member of Parliament who asked how many charges of assault were lodged against policemen in the years from 1953, how many policemen were prosecuted and how many were convicted, was told that 'the desired particulars are not readily available and can only be obtained by an enormous amount of additional research at each and every police station in the country'. Are allegations by the public that they have been assaulted by the police so many, or are they taken so casually, that details are not available at a level sufficiently high to make their collection a fairly simple matter?

(CT 2/7/59)

The newspaper described the situation as a 'Police emergency'.

And I remembered, too, that one evening in about 1954 I had sat at my own dining room table with a white member of the South African Police. He had come to my farm on police business, and we had invited him to stay for a meal. At table we were discussing cattle rustling, which was then prevalent in the British colony of Basutoland, yet hardly at all in the Orange Free State.

'How is it,' I asked him, 'that just over there, across the Caledon River, stock theft is so bad, yet here in the Free State there is so little of it?' Our guest, whose rank was Detective

Head Constable, said: 'That's an easy one to answer. Over here we don't let them keep the stolen stock.' I said: 'What do you mean? How do you find the stock? In Basutoland the trouble is that the thieves hide the stock within hours of stealing it.' He said: 'That's just it. Over here we make them tell us where they are.' 'How do you do that?' 'Well there are three ways. The first is that we hit them. The second is electric shocks. And the third is the gasmask. The shock usually works as they are terrified of electricity. But the gasmask always works. That way you put the gasmask over his head. Then you tell him that if he won't talk you'll stop the air going in so that he can't breathe. Then you stop the air. When he faints you let the air go in again and bring him round. Then you tell him that this time you were merciful. You brought him back from the other side. The next time, if he doesn't talk, you're going to let him stay there. When this happens they always talk.'

This man's name was Nieuwenhuis, and aside from his normal police duties he was watching the situation on behalf of the 'Gestapo', the security branch in Bloemfontein.

I also remembered that in 1959 businessmen in Cape Town complained that their secretaries could not work in offices near the police station at Caledon Square because of the 'pleadings and screams of people being beaten'. (N 27/6/59)

Statistics, too, have a bearing on the reputation of a police force. What do we find here?

January 1, 1949 – *April* 30, 1951
  347 police found guilty in court of assault, and 52 found guilty departmentally: 51 dismissed. Statement by the minister of justice in parliament. (S 22/6/51)
During 1952
  Figures for convictions of police in court:

Crimes of violence, 141

Crimes against prisoners in their charge, 41

Perjury, 7   Other offences, 732

Of the above there were dismissed, 94   (FT March 1953)

1953

Police convicted in court:

338 of various charges, in addition to

22 of offences against persons in their charge.

1954

450 of various charges.

The figures for 1953 and 1954 were given by the minister of justice, Charles Robberts Swart, to Alexander Hepple, M.P., in parliament. (S 27/1/58)

January 1, 1955 – *March* 1956

Police convicted of theft, 76

Of 'immorality', 3

Of assault, 308

Of homicide, 7

Of those convicted of assault, 226 were still in the force. The above information was given in parliament by the minister of justice. (F 17/3/56)

1957

Police convicted of various offences, 574*

Of crimes of violence, 139*

Of offences against prisoners in their charge, 80 (S 27/1/58)

1960

Police charged with assaulting prisoners in their charge, 566

Of whom there were convicted, 311

And of whom there were dismissed from the force, 11

(O 17/11/63)

---

*The report does not make it clear whether the 139 is included in, or in addition to, the 574.

MIN. SWART·SE KATS

1. When he became minister of justice, Charles Robberts Swart had himself photographed holding up a cat-o'-nine-tails, the official instrument of corporal punishment. This photograph appeared in the Cape Town nationalist daily *Die Burger*. Many of his interventions in the field of justice will be found in these pages, and it will be readily understood how suitably this photograph symbolizes the character of his administration. In particular, for the immense increase of corporal punishment due to his influence, see p. 133

2. Crowd control by the South African police is well illustrated in this photograph. In 1959, the police were dispersing a crowd of five thousand women demonstrating against the then control of home-brewing of beer. Since then the African people have been given legal access to alcohol.

The above is a tale of mounting harshness. For much of this harshness Swart must take responsibility. Early in his cabinet career he announced that he would protect 'his' force against those who criticized its ready use of sten-guns against the non-whites. And to deter people from reporting policemen who misbehaved he removed the numbers from the uniforms of the white members of the force. African, coloured, and other non-white policemen kept their numbers, which had always been previously worn by all members of the force.

Swart was made governor-general and, later, president in 1961, and a successor restored the practice whereby all, including white, policemen, wear identification numbers on their uniform. (CT 8/8/61)

Swart left a malodorous reputation at the department of justice. Under his control the Police force behaved more and more as a tribal impi* and less and less as the impartial maintainers of law and order. Sometimes the police were frankly racist. For instance, in 1955, one Fernando Kasumbila sued the minister of justice for £200 for wrongful arrest and assault. Evidence showed that he had been wantonly assaulted by the police. Released next morning from cells, no charge was laid. He complained to his white master. Together they went to the police station. 'His employer asked the policemen why they had hit him and one of them replied: "Because he is black and I am white".' (F 6/5/55)

People fear the vengeance of the police. A letter in *The Star* from a responsible social worker told how one man, born in Rhodesia, who had worked for one employer for 14 years, was arrested at night in his own room in Alexandra and was asked for his permit to live in Alexandra, and was thereafter assaulted. A lawyer was instructed to defend him, and the case was withdrawn. He laid a charge against the African constable who

*Regiment (Zulu).

C   33

had assaulted him, and judgment was given in his favour. The
constable was fined. The employee's permit to live in Alexandra was renewed – but he no longer lived in Alexandra,
because 'the police will get me'. The writer added: 'I assure
you that such arrests are frequent (of people who have committed no crime, and whose documents are in order). I have
taken up a number of such cases. . . . I shudder to think how
many there are . . . who are too timid to appeal'. (S 15/7/57)

The police acted as a tribal impi under Swart because he
unashamedly took the part of the white man in virtually every
case that went before him. As an example, in which incident-
ally the police were not implicated, in 1957 a white man who
owned a hotel in Wellington (Cape) committed a brutal assault
on a coloured man. He was convicted by a magistrate and sentenced to a fine of £50. The prosecution was not satisfied, and
the attorney-general appealed. The supreme court agreed with
the attorney-general, and increased the fine to £150. There
was also a prison sentence of two weeks. This was left unaltered
by the higher court, which knew, when it left the prison sentence alone, that the man would lose his liquor licence, and be
unable to keep his hotel business. Although the court made a
clear decision on this point, the government, acting on the
advice of Swart, pardoned the man in respect of the imprisonment. The pardon followed representations by a number of
white farmers, friends of the accused. (S 19/11/57)

It was Swart, too, who, when he was first made minister of
justice, had himself photographed holding a cat-o'-nine-tails,
the very symbol of brutal punishment. That photograph has
never been forgotten, particularly by the non-whites. Statistics
speak here too. In 1945, before the Swart period, 2,649 persons
received 15,767 strokes of corporal punishment in prison. But
in 1958, after Swart had legislated to make corporal punish-

ment mandatory in certain cases, 18,542 persons received 93,775 strokes. Thus is apartheid maintained!

Swart's occupation of the ministry of justice will never be forgotten. Here are some more statistics, also taken from the highly reputable Penal Reform League's information sheet:

1945 (pre-Swart)		1958 (after several years of Swart)
Daily average in prison	22,929	51,000 (approximately)
Youthful offenders in prison	10,802	24,174
Persons actually executed expressed as a percentage of those sentenced to death: i.e. percentage not granted clemency	29.3	63.1

Swart's reputation is bad. But let us not therefore exonerate the sytem. The reputation of the South African police, in their dealings with the non-whites, is a reputation of corruption, cruelty and terror.

It is now appropriate to examine some of the concrete cases that will justify my use of these strong words.

CHAPTER THREE
Torture
Found hanging in his cell

As mentioned earlier, a well-known leader of the Cape African National Congress, Looksmart Solwandle Ngudle, died in the hands of the police on or about September 5, 1963. The manner of his death was mysterious. The official story is that he was found hanged in his cell. But it was widely believed that he had been tortured, and possibly killed by the police. An attempt was made at the inquest to have the matter properly investigated, but the representative of the widow, Dr George Lowen, a distinguished member of the Johannesburg bar, withdrew when he realised that the law made it impossible for him to repeat statements by Ngudle because he was a banned person.

The matter had not, at the time of writing, been properly investigated, and several features of the case seemed suspicious.

Ngudle was detained on August 19 under the 90-day clause. According to the counsel for the government, V. Marinus, 'he was interrogated on a number of occasions. On the day before he was found dead he gave the police information that led to other arrests. . . . He realised he had given information which would lead to retribution from the persons concerned. It was a case of being put to death by the proper functions of the law or being put to death by the people with whom he had previously associated. That was his predicament'.

So much for the official point of view. It is admitted by them that Ngudle had been interrogated many times. He died sixteen days after being detained. Yet another ten days passed before the news of his death was given to his relatives. His mother, living at Middledrift, Cape, was told that her son had

36

'passed away'. When she asked how he had died, she was told that he had hanged himself. Her immediate reaction was one of disbelief. On 15th September she asked that his body be sent back home for burial, but this was refused on the grounds that it would be 'too expensive'. She went up to Pretoria, arriving on 22nd September. She went straight to the jail where the authorities first told her that they knew nothing of the matter. But later they told her that the body had been buried. They said it had been buried at the request of his wife, but she strenuously denied making any such request. The mother then asked for the clothes, but this, too, was refused. The authorities said there were no clothes. A post-mortem report on the death was made by a government doctor, Dr Loubser, but it was so inadequately done that medical men could not, from a perusal of it, determine whether death was by hanging or other cause, and that it did not help in establishing whether the hanging was before or after death. It was an incomplete report: it did not give the time of death, and the cause of death given, 'hanging', was an inference which need not be drawn from the facts. And there were other irregularities. (S 26/10/63)

At the inquest evidence was given by another person detained under the 90-day clause, Isaac Tlale. He had been held for 14 weeks in solitary confinement, and told the inquest court that he had been beaten by the police, forced to undress, and given an electric shock. He said that he himself was never allowed out of his cell, even for exercise, and that his food consisted of bread three times a day. He was hit on the head with part of a chair, grabbed round the neck, and kicked during an interrogation. After being given an electric shock he lost consciousness. The next thing he remembered was standing at a table signing a blank document headed with his name and address, with a policeman holding his hand. (G 28/11/63)

The Jassat case

There was an explosion in a railway tool-shed in Johannesburg on April 17, 1963. According to a statement issued by the Anti-apartheid Movement in London, a 29-year-old merchant, Abdulhay Jassat, was arrested, not at the scene of the explosion, but at his home at 3 a.m. by about fifteen police, on suspicion of having been connected with the explosion. He was taken first to the South African Police station at Marshall Square, then to the Railway Police station at Park Station, together with four other suspects.

He was kept for some hours in a room with a guard, and was later called out for interrogation by about twenty plain-clothes police who fired questions at him. Jassat refused to reply to them. Then the men put a canvas bag on him, covering almost his entire body, and tied it at his knees. They then suspended him by his legs and swung him about. After this his shoes and socks were taken off and wires were attached to his big toes, and electric charges applied with increasing intensity. All the time the police plied him with questions about the sabotage and about those involved with it. Water was poured over his feet, presumably to maximize conductivity.

After the electric torture he was made to stand on one foot with the other foot raised, and a pin was held under the raised foot. During all this torture Jassat screamed a great deal. The electric treatment lasted about an hour. They then made him do various exercises, beating him whenever he paused. He said: 'When they saw that I was almost finished they carried me away to another room as I could not walk. Later I could hear the cries of my friends'.

The friends were four other men of Indian origin named Chiba, Vandeyar, Nanabhai, and Naidoo. The first three had treatment similar to that given to Jassat. Naidoo had been shot on the scene of the explosion. He was shot from the front, the bullet entering at the shoulder.

Jassat was charged with sabotage, but the charge was later withdrawn. Immediately the charge was withdrawn he was re-arrested and detained under the 90-day clause. On the morning of August 10 he and three other members of the Congress movement, a political alliance which opposes apartheid, escaped from Marshall Square, and all four managed to get out of South Africa to safety. (*Sunday News*, Dar-es-Salaam, 22/9/63)

Earlier accounts of torture by electricity

In 1961 the Tembuland police were investigating the murder of a government-supporting headman Spalding Matyile and another collaborator William Ntambeka. They rounded up at one stage all the able-bodied men in eleven locations (villages). At the subsequent preparatory examination before a magistrate two crown witnesses contradicted statements they had earlier made to the police on the grounds that they had been beaten and tortured with electricity. One witness, Gawuleteta Rabula, described being taken to the stables behind the Engcobo jail, being blindfolded, and being given electrical shocks on his feet. The second witness, Matekana Mduna, showed a small wound above his right temple which he said had been caused by a nail which penetrated his scalp when he was thrown to the ground by the force of an electrical shock. And a third witness, Lewis Majija, a teacher of 24 years' service, quoted the actual words used to him by a policeman, Sgt De Beer, who threatened him before applying electricity to his body: 'I am going to reduce your weight by ten pounds in two seconds'. Majija is a heavily-built man. (C 25/2/61)

In 1956 the police at Boshof, Orange Free State, were investigating a case of shopbreaking and theft. They wanted to make a 17-year-old lad, Daniel Motshwaro, confess to the crime. They were said to have beaten him with a sjambok (rhino-hide whip), given him an electric shock, and held his face near a glowing stove. The assailants, whites and Africans, were all police.

Motshwaro said that on June 22 Geldenhuys and Motaung took him from school to a garage at the Boshof police station. Geldenhuys told him he would not be charged if he confessed to breaking into a shop and if the police recovered stolen money.

Motshwaro said he had not broken into the shop. Geldenhuys then told Motaung to bring a sjambok and a motor-car fan belt.

The boy then added that Geldenhuys told Motaung to close the door. He ordered Motshwaro to take off his coat. Geldenhuys hit him hard many times with the sjambok.

The Native constable hit him with the fan belt as he tried to escape the sjambok blows. Mothswaro said that after the beating he denied breaking into the shop.

He then had to lie on gravel on the concrete floor of the garage holding his hands above his head. He was left in this position for a while, he said.

Calitz then arrived and struck him on the head.

After Motshwaro had been blindfolded, he said he felt shocks, which shook his bound hands violently.

The cloth was taken from his eyes, and Calitz hit him on the nose, causing it to bleed. He saw Calitz carrying an object connected to electric wires. He was then taken out of the garage to wash, as his nose was bleeding.

Geldenhuys and Els, he said, then hit him many times Els then hit him with a cane three times. Geldenhuys, Calitz, Els, Motaung, Moloi and Dammie stood round Motshwaro, and all hit him from side to side.

'When I fell they picked me up, and hit me down again,' he said.

(S 24/1/56)

In 1957 the police tried to get information from one Sergeant Nyoni at Hlobane, Natal. As a result a policeman, Gideon Petrus Opperman, and a butcher, Paul Johannes Fick, were charged with assault. They pleaded guilty.

> They were alleged to have shocked Nyoni with electricity, to have hit him on the soles of his feet with a cane and an iron bar, and to have banged his head on the ground and against a desk.
>
> Nyoni showed the court an inch-thick scar which circled his left leg just above the ankle. He also showed a broken line of scars on his calf. He said the scars were caused by the electricity burning him when Opperman and Fick shocked him as he lay spread-eagled on a table in the Hlobane police station.
>
> Native Cons. Isiah Tabete said he saw Opperman and Fick 'putting electricity into Nyoni.' He went into a rondavel in which were Opperman, Fick and Nyoni.
>
> Nyoni was spread over a table, with his arms and legs fastened to the table leg with handcuffs and foot manacles.
>
> One end of a length of electric flex was fastened about one of Nyoni's legs and the other was plugged into the electric light socket.
>
> Constable Tabete said that when he was there Opperman said 'Switch on' to Fick. Fick turned on the current. Nyoni's body jerked and he shouted. The current was switched on only a moment and then switched off.
>
> (A 17/6/58)

A further detail in this case was added by *Die Burger*, Cape Town's nationalist newspaper. The witness was reported as saying that the assailants were drinking, and took turns to turn the current on and off. They laughed as the current produced spasms in his body. It is of interest that the voltage used in South Africa is not 110 volts, as used in America, but is the far more dangerous 220-230 volt system that frequently kills people accidentally.

In 1962 a witness in a case of robbery told a court in Johannesburg: 'I was electrocuted and assaulted and forced to make the statement. Then I was afraid to report it (meaning the assault)'. (RDM 17/5/62)

In 1955 the police in East London were investigating a case of theft. A quantity of kaffir sheeting (coarse cloth) had been stolen from a factory at Chiselhurst.

One witness, Dickson Bazi, said that he had been questioned at Duncan Village charge office. During the questioning a policeman named Sergeant Matthys assaulted him. 'He was also shocked with an electric cable. The cable was wound round a finger on each hand. . . . A mask was then placed over his head. It suffocated him. When he was given the electric shock he was hurled against a wall and received a bruise on the right temple.' (F 12/1/56)

In 1957 two Afrikaner policemen (one a detective-sergeant named Johannes Christoffel du Preez) were charged in court with assaulting one Isaac Radebe 'by undressing him, hanging him upside-down from a pole passed through his arms and legs, passing an electric current through his handcuffs, hitting him with a plank through which a nail was driven, and hitting and kicking him'. The medical evidence was that the right eyebrow was lacerated, and that there was an abrasion on the leg. (S 30/7/57)

Torture without electricity

So much for torture in which electricity forms an element. Here are some other cases with other forms of torture: forcing a victim to kneel and hold a chair above his head, and tightening the screws on handcuffs, permanently maiming his hands (CT 25/8/61). Assaulting an African woman prisoner by flinging

a hosepipe round her neck, almost throttling her, and assaulting her while she was unconscious. Found guilty, the police
responsible were each fined £3 or seven days' hard labour.
(F 5/7/52)

'His left ear hanging'
One of the most fearful killings by torture occurred after a
white farmer, of Leliekloof farm, Cradock district, Cape, was
killed at night in his own home, on January 13, 1959.

On January 16 the police arrived at the farm and took
Moyisi Sikaka away for questioning. Sikaka was a worker
on the farm.

Sikaka died the next day, January 17, while in police
custody.

The relatives were informed of his death a day later, on
January 18.

Sikaka's wife saw the coffin on a human ordure lorry and
accompanied it to the graveyard.

When she and relatives were refused permission to see
the body or to arrange for its burial themselves, they approached an attorney.

Sworn statements were obtained that Sikaka had been
assaulted by the police before his death.

Two affidavits are on record from Angelina (his wife).

In the first, she said that nothing had happened to her
husband.

In the second, however – which resulted subsequently in
her being charged with perjury – she said that the police
beat and kicked and trampled on her husband shortly before he died.

She said that she saw her husband with his face covered
with blood and his left ear 'hanging'. He kept opening his
mouth without saying anything.

Angelina alleged that the police hit her husband on the

43

head with handcuffs, and then took him to an adjoining room and assaulted him again.

After her husband's death, the police told her that the cause of death had been heart failure.

Other sworn statements have been made supporting the allegation of assault by the police on Sikaka.

At the inquest the Cradock Magistrate, Mr M. S. Hough, found that Sikaka died as a result of sub-cranial haemorrhage probably caused when he fell several times during a police search for a safe in a murder investigation.

The law governing inquests prevented the attorney representing the family from calling witnesses or from addressing the court on the merits of the case.

Subsequently the attorney applied to the Attorney-General for an order for the body to be exhumed.

(ST 22/3/59)

But the attorney-general and the minister of justice, Swart, decided not to allow an exhumation.

This case was courageously taken up by Senator Leslie Rubin, of the Liberal Party, with the minister. He pointed out that the dead man's relatives were informed of his death an hour before the police buried him; that no relatives were allowed to see the body; that an exhumation order was refused; and that minister Swart refused to answer any questions in the senate on the grounds that the case against others for killing the farmer was *sub judice*. (ST 22/3/59)

Buried on a beach

Another fearful killing was reported from Zululand in 1955. Two sergeants of the South African Police, Bentley van Eck, aged 30, and Joachim Christoffel Potgieter, aged 25, were charged for killing a prisoner, Mgawuli Ndhlovu, aged 18, who had been in their charge.

They suspected Ndhlovu of storebreaking and theft. For two

44

days they flogged and kicked him in an attempt to get him to show them where the stolen goods had been hidden. They threatened to burn him with 'electric'. In the end he died.

The assaults began on Monday, November 7. Van Eck thrashed Ndhlovu and another African with a strip of motor tyre. Van Eck forced the two men to hold a brick in each hand, and to hold the bricks above their heads while they were thrashed. At the same time he asked them to point out where the goods were hidden. That afternoon Ndhlovu was assaulted by both accused. He was handcuffed to the bumper of a van, and crept under the vehicle in an attempt to avoid the blows, one of which broke the left front lamp of the van. Van Eck, it is alleged, reversed the van. It went over Ndhlovu. Then Potgieter thrashed him.

On the Tuesday morning Ndhlovu was sent out with two African police to look for the goods. Some evidence existed that these two African police also assaulted Ndhlovu.

On the Tuesday afternoon Van Eck and Potgieter went out again with Ndhlovu and the other African suspect. Potgieter threatened that he would burn the other African with 'electric' if he did not show them where the goods had been hidden. Van Eck then assaulted Ndhlovu in a plantation. Then he was handcuffed to a tree. Then, in the words of the prosecutor, 'a very serious assault took place'. The two sergeants had by this time completely lost their tempers. They thrashed Ndhlovu. When the one was tired the other took over the thrashing. They thrashed him all over his body and booted him. Ndhlovu then collapsed. According to one witness, blood issued from his nose and he urinated blood. Then the sergeants struck him again. Then they saw he was dead.

When they saw he was dead they had a discussion about what to do. The body was placed on the van and at the Kwambonambi police station an African was instructed to spray the body with a hose. It was buried in a plantation. Later the two sergeants dug it up and buried it on the beach at Kwambonambi.

In an attempt to cover up their tracks they staged a fake search for Ndhlovu, who, they pretended, had run away. They sent two African constables on patrol duty to search for Ndhlovu. The African constables pretended to go out in a certain direction but once they were out of sight of the sergeants they changed their direction and went to Empangeni. They reported what they had seen to the police there. (S.6, 8/2/56)

Piet tried to crawl away
Piet Machika was a farm labourer in the notorious Delmas district of the Transvaal. On July 28, 1959, a 20-year-old white constable, Antonie Stefanus de Bruto, approached Machika on the farm Witklip. We are not told why he approached Machika. But he grabbed him by the shirt front and hit him several blows on the body with his fist. When the man pulled away from the constable's grip his jacket was pulled off and his shirt torn.

An African witness reported to his white master that a police constable was assaulting a farm labourer. The master said: 'That is not our business. Just ignore what is going on'.

Machika was then knocked down and tried to crawl away on his hands and knees. The constable grabbed him by the arm and another struggle followed during which he was again struck by the constable. During the scuffle, Machika was thrown to the ground. The constable sat on top of him, gave him another beating, and handcuffed him.

The constable got up and, while Machika was still, lying on the ground, smacked him across the face with the flat of his hand and then hauled him to his feet. He staggered a few paces, fell flat on his face, and never got up again.

46

While the assault was going on, a few white men watched from a nearby shop. They did nothing till Machika was knocked out. Then they got into a car and drove to the scene of the assault and helped the constable to load the man into the back of the car. They drove to Delmas, followed by De Bruto on his bicylce.

That night Machika's body was identified at the police station. (CT 14/11/59)

The last case which I wish to quote is another case in which a prisoner died. Sergeant John Victor De Bruyn, and Constable Stephanus Johannes Marais, were charged in June 1962 with culpable homicide. The assault arose out of an investigation of a reported loss of £45. They interrogated one James Sondesi. It was alleged that while he was questioning Sondesi Marais pressed handcuffs against the prisoner's wrists, till Sondesi complained of the pain. Later Marais hit him at the Nqutu charge office with his open hand. Then De Bruyn hit him with his open hand. Every time they hit him his head banged up against the cupboard behind him. Both men grabbed Sondesi and banged his head against the cupboard. They did this in turn.

Later Sondesi's face was seen to be swollen and he was staggering. One Nsibande told him to sit down: 'I thought there was something wrong with him and he told me that his head was aching'. Later he heard De Bruyn tell someone to say that Sondesi had fallen from the van. Sondesi died on March 8. (RDM 16/6/62)

To complete this account, incomplete though it is, of torture by the South African Police, I quote an exchange in the Senate between Senator Rall of the United Party, who is an ex-magistrate, and Balthasar Johannes Vorster, at present minister of justice of South Africa. Senator Rall told the minister that third-degree methods were already being used by the police.

47

He knew this from his own experience. Many a day when he was on the bench someone appeared before him with a bloody face and accused the police of having manhandled him, upon which the police always said that he resisted arrest.

Vorster: What did you do about it?

Senator Rall said that he had been able to do little. But in one case as a result of his objections about a certain policeman always bullying suspects, the policeman was transferred to the north coast of Natal. Soon after Senator Rall had left the government service the same policeman was charged with the brutal murder of a suspect, and was sentenced to $6\frac{1}{2}$ years' imprisonment. Vorster's predecessor, Swart, had seen fit to release that man after six months and make him a warder in a prison.

Senator Rall also said that the police were using third-degree methods on a wide scale in their country-wide searches for firearms among Africans.

The minister's reaction was typical: 'Senator Rall saw fit to make certain references to me personally. I treat his remarks with the utter contempt which they deserve. That also applies to his despicable remarks about the police.' (S 1/5/63)

3. Crowd control by the South African police culminated, on March 21, 1960, in the massacre at Sharpeville when 69 people were killed. Here is one of the victims, shot from the back. See p. 67.

4. After Sharpeville the South African police went
through the homes of the African people, beating
them up, and trying to get them to return to work.
Here is an example dramatically photographed at
Langa, Cape Town, on April 4, 1960.

Four Unforgettable Cases

The Jooma Killing by Gideon Johannes Visser (the beast)

In December 1954 Constable Gideon Johannes Visser of the South African Police, stationed at Fordsburg, Johannesburg, arrested three men named Moosa, Patel, and Suliman Ismael Jooma. He charged them with disturbing the peace, resisting arrest and assaulting the police. And he charged Jooma with hindering the police in the execution of their duty. Suliman ('Solly') Jooma was a prominent political anti-apartheid leader, and a member of the Transvaal Indian Congress. Jooma and Patel were acquitted, and the charges against Moosa were withdrawn.

In February 1955, Visser received claims for £1,500 from the three men, and there were other claims against the minister of justice for £7,500. The action was set down for hearing in March 1956.

On the night of January 13, 1956, Visser was driving through Fordsburg with three others. In an underpass they saw Solly Jooma. Visser said: 'That is the man who is claiming £5,000 from me'. He turned the car and drove up to Jooma. Visser got out and hit Jooma, who fell to the ground. He then kicked him savagely. Then he felt for Jooma's pulse, and found that his heart had stopped. On his own statement Visser 'hacked his forehead with the heel of my boot so that the detectives would think he was assaulted by Natives'.

Then they drove off. A little later they returned. Visser looked at the body and said: 'He's dead'. About ten days later Visser asked a friend to clean some blood off his shoes. The friend asked where the blood came from, and Visser said: 'Don't you know I killed that Indian?' And a month or two later another witness heard Visser saying that he would fix anyone who said anything to him about the death of Jooma. (S 29/3/56)

Visser was charged with murder. Judge Rumpff sentenced Visser to ten years' imprisonment. In sentencing him the judge said: 'You are a beast. You are one of the most unsuitable people to wear a police uniform'.

How true those remarks were was borne out by Visser's reputation. He was a wild liver, gambler, and drinker.

Yet Visser did not serve those ten years. The judge forgot about the minister of justice, Charles Robberts Swart, who was later promoted to be governor-general and president, the head of state of the republic. The minister arranged it that Visser was moved to Cape Town for 'medical treatment'. This 'medical treatment' meant that he could walk round Cape Town a free man. No one could ever accuse Swart of dishonouring his early pledge to look after 'his boys'. And the fact that Swart was selected to be the president speaks much for the character of the apartheid state.

Mercy of a similar kind was shown to two white police sergeants, sentenced on February 25, 1956 in the Durban supreme court to imprisonment for eight and five years for killing an African prisoner. The two were released on the order of minister Swart on June 28, 1957. A condition was made that for a period of three years following their release they should not be found guilty of a crime of violence. This information was given in parliament by the minister of justice. (S 28/1/58)

Killing by water

The South African police are imaginative. Not even their worst enemies can accuse them of being dull creatures, tied to routine. And so they vary constantly the ways in which they torture and kill. They have even revived the medieval torture of forcing the victim to drink huge quantities of water. In this way they killed a sixteen-year-old boy named Leziwe Gwala. And as a result Constable Johannes Cornelius van Zyl was charged with culpable homicide and common assault.

The doctor's evidence was that the youth had been brought to him by three policemen in a police van for urgent attention. 'When first seen,' said the doctor, Dr Arthur Greenberg, 'Gwala was lying in the van, and I noticed a considerable quantity of blood-stained froth and fluid coming from his nostrils while he was being carried in. He was placed on the surgery table and I listened to his heart. The beat was still audible. I began artificial respiration and told Van Zyl (one of the police) to continue it, while I gave Gwala a heart stimulant in the arm muscle. I refilled the syringe for an intravenous injection, but found the vein in the arm had collapsed. I listened to his heart, but it had stopped beating. . . . Gwala was dead.'

Dr Greenberg said that when Gwala was first brought to him a report was made that he had drunk a quantity of water, and that he had collapsed. One of the policemen made this report.

The next day the doctor held a post-mortem in the presence of a senior medical officer in a nearby big town, Pietermaritzburg. 'The appearance of the dead umfaan (youth) . . . (was) . . . what I would have expected in a case of drowning. . . . In my opinion, one gallon of water would have been excessive for a person of Gwala's size. The excess distention would cause considerable discomfort and pain and would induce a state of shock. He would have feelings of pain, feeling cold, shivering, and perspiration. . . . The eyes were swollen in a manner consistent with being struck in the face with a fist.'

Another witness, Magwaza Biyela, who was with Gwala at the police station on November 19, said Gwala shivered and staggered on the way to a lavatory after leaving the European constable, and that he told an African constable and sergeant: 'They gave me water to drink'. (S 31/1/51)

The quartering of Willie Smit

Another medieval practice that is receiving a latter-day revival in South Africa is the practice of killing by quartering. In the old days the worst malefactors would be executed by having a horse attached to each limb, and the horses driven off in different directions. For some three hundred years Europe has allowed this barbarous practice to lapse. But even this torture has been revived by the ingenious South African Police. For in 1958 they killed an elderly man named Willie Smit by stretching him between two lorries. It is hardly necessary to say that Willie Smit was not white: he was what they call a 'coloured man'.

As in so many similar cases the matter arose out of suspected theft. In some way suspicion descended on Willie Smit, and in October 1958, on the farm Glacis, belonging to Athelstone Henry Verran, a farmer, in the Cathcart district of the Cape Province, the police conducted an inquisition on Willie Smit, his son Stokkies Smit, and another man named Maxini Joko.

The police and the farmer perpetrated a series of assaults, over a period of four days, on the three victims.

Willie Smit was hung up in a tree, upside down, and severely beaten with sjamboks by Constable Michiel Jacobus Swart in the presence of Verran. Stokkies Smit was hung up too, and thrashed. Swart tied Stokkies Smit's hands in front of him, while another policeman pulled the rope over a branch. He was kept like that a little while. He was beaten with sjamboks, and with a piece of wood which had had the inner tube of a motor tyre wrapped round it.

Then Willie Smit promised to take the police to where he said they would find stolen goods. They loaded Willie Smit on

52

to a lorry, and drove to where he indicated. When they got there no stolen goods could be found. Then the two policemen put leg irons on Willie Smit's ankles and tied one leg iron to the bumper of a truck and the other leg iron to another truck. One of the policemen, Sergeant Philip Theunis de Wet Nel, then jumped into one of the trucks and began to reverse. Willie Smit screamed that he 'was being torn apart', one of the witnesses said. After the torture he was unable to speak. The police then untied him, and took him back to the police station, at Henderson, near Cathcart. After four days Willie Smit died. The doctors said he died of pneumonia, but they admitted that they could not say whether he died from the pneumonia or from the assaults. They found numerous bruises and abrasions on the body, and agreed that these might have contributed to his death.

And, speaking about the injuries that he found on Willie Smit's son, Stokkies Smit, Dr G. R. Howes, District Surgeon, Cathcart, said: 'If his injuries had been caused by assaults, then the assaults must have been severe and multiple'.

The police torturers were found guilty of assault with intent to do grievous bodily harm, and not of homicide or murder. (CT 21/3/59, 14/5/59: A 13/5/59)

The way the South African Police treated two Bushmen
Of all the peoples of South Africa the Bushmen (San people) are probably the most harmless. They withdrew into the Kalahari desert when stronger tribes moved into South Africa. There they live today, asking only to be left alone. They are tiny. Many of the grown-ups are no more than 4 feet high. They know little about the outside world. Occasionally the outer world bursts in on them, as will be seen. In 1962 a strange case was heard at Grootfontein, South West Africa. It is better left in the actual words of the *Cape Times* report of April 4.

GROOTFONTEIN. – Two European policemen were found guilty and a Native constable was found not guilty when the three appeared in the Magistrate's Court yesterday on charges of assault and incitement to commit crime.

Constable John Thomas Brits was found guilty on both charges and was fined a total of £40. Sergeant Karel de Wet Burger was found guilty of assault and fined £10. Native Constable Seth Gaugrob was found not guilty of both charges.

Evidence was that Burger, Brits and a party of police arrested a party of Bushmen alleged to have committed stock theft. They assaulted two of the Bushmen and the wife of one of the Bushmen with a hosepipe.

Later, they forced a Bushman to have relations with the Bushman woman. It was stated that although the Bushman woman and the Bushman lay down together no relations took place, in spite of Brits's orders. – (Sapa.) (CT 4/4/62)

On April 17 Mrs Helen Suzman, sole representative of the Progressive Party, took the matter up in parliament, as appears from a question and answer recorded thus in column 4094 of Hansard:

Mrs. Suzman asked:
Whether the two policemen who, according to a report in the *Cape Times* of 4 April, 1962, were found guilty of assault upon two Bushmen and a Bushman woman have been dismissed from the Police Force; and, if not, why not?
The MINISTER OF JUSTICE:
No. The matter is still being considered.

And that was that.

CHAPTER FIVE

Police Corruption

The 'protection racket', looting, rape, theft, 'immorality' and using government money to frequent brothels. . . . Surely not by a *police* force?

Nothing is too much for the South African police. Here are the facts:

Looting

Looting is not normally associated with the activities of a police force. Yet, after Sharpeville, in 1960, it was universally believed that the squads of police that were instructed to go through the 'locations' beating-up people who were staying away from work did not stop at physical persecution: they were believed to have stolen goods that took their fancy. In parliament, Cape Town, on May 18, the following remarks were made by L. B. Lee-Warden (Cape Western):

> Mr. Lee-Warden said that he and his parliamentary colleagues had been approached by many employers and told of cases of looting.
> Amounts ranging from £80 down had been stolen.
> GOVERNMENT MEMBERS: 'Stolen by whom?'
> 'Stolen by the police,' said Mr Lee-Warden.
> MR ERASMUS (Minister of Justice): 'Isn't that a shocking statement to make?'
> Mr Lee-Warden stated that about 2,000 police had taken part in room-to-room searches when they raided the quarters of about 20,000 Africans at Langa.
> They broke open every suit-case and box. They said they were searching for dangerous weapons. That was when the pilfering occurred.
> The raids for dangerous weapons might have been justified, but if they had been carried out under correct super-

55

vision 'this pilfering and looting would not have gone on'.
GOVERNMENT MEMBERS: 'We don't believe it.'

Mr Lee-Warden said that if Mr Erasmus wanted to clear the name of the police he should appoint a magistrate to investigate the allegations.

Mr Lee-Warden declared that many people had gone to the police and complained of the looting but they had been chased away.

'Now we have the real police state" declared Mr Lee-Warden.

Amid further protests from the Government benches he added: 'I have made these allegations from affidavits which I have taken.'

Referring to the police action against Langa residents when the township was cordoned off by the Army, Mr Lee-Warden said: 'The police went to Langa to beat up the people and chase them out to work.'

Mr Lee-Warden claimed that senior Defence Force officers had sought an interview with the chief of police and had threatened to withdraw their forces unless the violence stopped. (CT 19/5/60)

Some of the people who believed the police had looted were unwise enough to protest to the police. One of them, Alfred Maqubela, wrote about looting and about what happened when he tried to get £15 back:

Dear Sir,

I am very sorry, I would like to come and see you myself, but I can't. Here is the reason. At Langa I live in the Flats: there are three of us in one room, and I am the first to get there on Fridays. Last Friday I found the room open. I went in: everything was so upside down that I didn't know where to start. The pots, plates, spoons and that sort of thing were near the door. The first thing I did was to look at the suitcases, and I found that there was no money in them: before there had been about £15.

Ten minutes later another occupant came. He is a business man who sells new clothes from the wholesaler. He couldn't find his whole suitcase full of clothes.

And we were hungry; we always cook very early in the morning, and they had eaten all our supper. We had to start cooking again.

We locked the door and went to the Police Station to make a report. On the way we found a lot of our local friends and they told us that the police there were beating them so they ran away.

I said to the other man 'Let's go. Nothing will happen. I want my money.' When we got there they started beating us and I said that they could shoot me but I want my money. We went away. The police just looked at us and gave no answer.

Many people at Langa have had things stolen: suits, money and other things.

I don't mind giving my name, because this is true.

Thanks a lot for the help.

ALFRED MAQUBELA
(C 7/5/60)

The 'protection racket'

In September 1957 there were serious riots in the western areas of Johannesburg. The city council appointed a commission of inquiry. The commissioners were three former judges, the Hon A. van de Sandt Centlivres (a former chief justice of South Africa), the Hon L. Greenberg, and the Hon E. R. Roper.

Three respected members of the African community were among the witnesses. They said:

that gangsters in Alexandra township had indulged in their crimes, with the connivance of some members of the police force, for many years before the big clean-up there recently and the smashing of the Msomi and Spoiler gangs.

57

Mr Centlivres: Why should policemen help these criminals?

A witness: 'They share the spoils.'

The commission was told that several European and non-European police sergeants were relieved of their duties in Alexandra during the recent clean-up.

A witness said one of the worst Native criminals of all time was given weapons and ammunition by the police for his work in trying to break the Evaton bus boycott.

It was alleged that this man was employed to break the boycott.

Mr Roper: 'Is there any evidence that this is true?' – 'He was convicted and he told the court these things.'

'When we hear and read such things,' the witness said, 'we feel helpless.'

Mr A. Douglas Davidson, who is leading the evidence: Is there a common general feeling among Africans that the police are in league with the criminals? – 'Yes.'

'There are some outstanding criminals who are never touched. If they are pointed out to the police, no one ever knows what happens to the charge.'

A memorandum submitted by three witnesses, stated: 'Although the police are necessary for the maintenance of peace and order in the community, in African urban townships they have proved a failure.

'Not only are they hated by the people for their unfriendly, ruthless attitude, but they are also despised for their methods of dealing with a situation which requires careful handling.

'The Department of Justice, in employing police, should consider age, place of birth and standard of education achieved by the individual rather than employ young arrogant men from the rural areas who hate to see an educated urban African.' (S 25/2/58)

Rape and indecent assault

In about 1957 Jacobus Ernst Retief, aged 20, a former constable in the South African Police, stationed at Point, Durban, was sentenced to four years' imprisonment and six strokes by Mr Acting Justice Bizzell in the Supreme Court, Durban, for raping an African woman whom he had arrested under the curfew (pass) regulations on the night of January 24.

It was said that Retief resigned from the police. (CT date unrecorded)

'We cried tears'

Police vans in South Africa are called 'pick-up vans'. The description is occasionally all too accurate, as appeared from the case in which Constable Gerhardus Jacobus van der Ryst (aged 22) was charged with raping two African girls (one of whom was aged 13) in the police barracks at Springs.

This young girl said:

> that she and her sister, with their parents and an aunt, were walking from Springs Railway Station towards Payneville Native Township on the evening of November 3. They were on their way to church.
>
> Before they reached Payneville a police van passed them, stopped and reversed. Van der Ryst got out and asked her father for their passes. He was alone.
>
> 'The policeman ordered my sister and me to get into the van. My aunt wanted to get in with us, but he said he would take us to the church later.
>
> 'The door was shut. The van went off and we stopped behind a large building. There Van der Ryst opened the door, ordered us out and kissed me. Then he pushed us back into the van and shut us in.
>
> 'Quite a long time after he returned and put his arms about us. We walked to the large building. He saw some people coming and told us to run back to the van. There

59

he kissed both of us and, after looking round the corner, told us to go back to the building.'

Mr D. J. Curlewis (for the Crown): What did you think he was going to do? – We thought he was going to lock us up.

Van der Ryst ordered them to go upstairs. When they stopped he said: 'Did you not hear me? If you do not go I will shoot you.'

He again threatened them when they hesitated at the door of a room upstairs. There he ordered them to undress. Van der Ryst also undressed.

Then he assaulted her sister and herself.

Mr Curlewis: Why did you not cry out? – We cried tears. Van der Ryst said that if we cried out aloud he would kill us.

(S 25/3/52)

And, in June 1957 Detective-Sergeant Daniel Blignaut, stationed at Umbilo, Durban, indecently assaulted a young African woman who he had taken to the Umbilo police station in connection with another case. He was fined £30. (S 18/6/57)

Theft

Three police broke into an outhouse at Blouvlei, Retreat, Cape Town, on October 19, 1958, and stole the carcase of a slaughtered cow. An 18-year-old police constable stole a bicycle in his charge at Roodepoort, Transvaal. (CT 12/6/59, A 14/3/59.) And a 19-year-old constable, H. G. Martins, stole from an African clergyman a briefcase containing a hymn book, a fountain pen, and a bottle of wine. (D 10/5/59)

'Immorality'

'Immorality' has been given inverted commas, not because there is no immorality in South Africa, but because the 'Immorality Act' together with the 'Mixed Marriages Act', make nonsense of the normal meaning of the word. It is illegal now in South Africa for any white person to have sexual intercourse with any non-white person, whether within wedlock or out of wedlock. On the other hand, as far as the law goes, there is no discouragement of immorality of any kind, so long as it is not across the colour line. 'Immorality', however, is illegal, and the law is stringently enforced. Police spy on people at night, in their own and other homes, and, above all, in parked motor cars.

But this is not to say that the police do not themselves practise 'immorality'. They do, and on a great scale. Their unique opportunities have a good deal to do with this state of affairs. And so does the old maxim about forbidden fruit being sweeter.

Thus, within 31 days in 1959, in one city, Cape Town, there were convictions in three cases in which policemen were prosecuted for 'immorality'. It is not necessary to go into the details of these cases, except to make it clear that this law was made by apartheid, and that apartheid puts people in the situation where a police uniform gives a man excessive power over voteless people. (CT 21/3/59, 18/4/59, 21/4/59)

Brothels
It is an old custom in the South African Police that the fullest use is made of the 'agent-provocateur' or trap. That is to say, if the police suspect that someone is trading in diamonds illegally, they will dress a policeman up as someone looking as though he wanted to trade illegally in diamonds, and try to persuade the suspect to trade. If he agrees, the policeman whips his disguise off, produces his identity card, and arrests the illicit diamond buyer.

This practice has paid good dividends for the police over many years, and so, with their accustomed ingenuity, they have extended the field of activities for their agents-provocateurs. The latest field to be explored is that of brothels or so-called 'friendship clubs'.

In 1959 a 33-year-old model, a bachelor of arts, was charged with keeping a brothel at her flat during March. The principal evidence against her was that of a detective. He testified that he had been given her address by another woman who ran a 'friendship club', and that he had gone to her flat, and had a drink with her. He then gave her £10, and they thereupon had sexual intercourse. A week later he went with two other detectives to her flat to arrest her.

Proceedings revealed that the £10 was government money. It later became clear that this field of police activity had become popular, and another case, at about the same time, was brought against a 24-year-old divorcee under the same law. In all there were six cases: a considerable number of police used public money in such visits.

Earlier requests for inquiries into police misbehaviour had all been turned down by the minister of justice, Charles Robberts Swart. But this time, with his mind no doubt on the Committee on Social Evils of the Dutch Reformed Church, he ordered an immediate inquiry. (CT, B 8/5/59)

Not all these examples of corruption affect the enforcement of white supremacy directly. But corruption is no respecter of races, and the sufferings of the voteless are greater because the South African Police is corrupt than they would be if the force were incorrupt.

CHAPTER SIX

The Frightened Children

African children are terrified of the South African Police, especially of the white South African Police. They have reason to be. Here are some of the happenings reported to the *Sunday Times* by C. E. Poulton, a farmer of the farm Piva, near Kaapmuiden, Transvaal: On June 28, 1961, Colin Poulton, the nine-year-old son of the farmer, was playing at the farm dam with a group of African children, whose average age was about seven years. Suddenly a number of policemen (who came from a distant police station) arrived, and rounded up the African children, and marched them down to a stream which runs under the railway. The white boy, Colin, was very frightened, and fled to his home.

The group of African children was taken down to some pools in the stream. They were asked where their parents hid their *dagga* (marihuana). When the frightened children said that they knew nothing about it, they were beaten about the head with a cane as thick as a finger. The police then grabbed one of the children named Boy Mondhlani, and made him lie down. Then they lifted him by his heels and let his head dangle in one of the pools of water. Weeping in terror, he was then allowed to stand. Then the police told the children to run. They did so, and as they ran a revolver shot was fired. The bullet struck the road near them. These children, and Colin Poulton, were so frightened by all this that for a week the parents could do nothing with them.

One white constable whose name was not given, was responsible for all this. On the same occasion and on the same farm he maimed a man for life.

The incident began with the visit of an African to the farm Piva. He was dressed in civilian clothes. He told the African farm workers that he wanted to buy dagga. They recognised him as a man who had worked in Kaapmuiden, and who was known to be a dagga pedlar. They told him they did not wish to deal in dagga. He then said he was a policeman, and tried to kick the door of a hut open. The labourers did not believe that he was a policeman, seized him, and locked him in a concrete storeroom at the packhouse pending the farmer's return. During the scuffle one of the labourers named Sweet Matsoni smacked this 'pedlar-policeman'. Then this large group of policemen arrived, released this man, and took him to a compound where a white constable asked him to point out the man who had struck him. He pointed out Matsoni. Matsoni dodged behind a hut. Finding his escape cut off by the constable on one side of the hut and the police on the other, he tried to make a dash for it. One of the white constables shot him in the back.

This posse then departed, taking the wounded Matsoni with them.

The farmer, Poulton, was not able to follow up his servant, Matsoni: 'In the rush of the harvest season I could only hope that the police were doing what was right with Matsoni. When, on July 21, I got a bill from the Barberton hospital for the customary 5s I decided to investigate, as the information I had been able to get was unsatisfactory. I drove 28 miles across the mountains to Barberton. I was told by the hospital there that Matsoni had been 'discharged'. I then went to put the whole matter before Major Grobbelaar, the district commandant (of police) in Nelspruit. It was only when he made inquiries that it was discovered that Sweet Matsoni was lying in hospital in Pretoria, paralysed from the waist down'. (ST 30/7/61.) Later the attorney-general of the Transvaal, R. W. Rein, gave instructions that the constable in question should be prosecuted. (CT 1/8/61)

At the market in Bloemfontein

Children have been frightened by the South African Police more than once. In 1959 *Contact*, a liberal fortnightly, was sent a report from Bloemfontein which indicated how the large, adult white police there kept the small boys near the market in order:

> From time to time children in Bloemfontein find themselves before the magistrates charged with minor pilfering from market stalls, begging in the streets, annoying white motorists or perhaps committing a nuisance at the municipal market by importuning white women to allow them to carry their baskets.
>
> The crime may often be as trifling as romping on the pavements near the market, thus causing 'obstruction' to well-fed farmers and well-loaded housewives in a hurry to get home with their abundant purchases.
>
> It is customary for magistrates to sentence such unhappy delinquents to cuts with a light cane. So far as can be gathered the number of cuts ranges between 3 and 12.
>
> Recently a child, grey with fright and hunger, broke a window but could not prove that he did so by mistake. He received a sentence of 4 cuts. Miscreants who purloin a bicycle pump or a tin of jam may get as many as 12 cuts.
>
> It has not been beyond the imagination of the South African Prisons Service to devise a method of carrying out the corporal punishment ordered by the Courts on these poor children caught up in the social squeeze of Bloemfontein. A batch of probably about a dozen youngsters shivering with fright in summer and both cold and fright in winter, are assembled in a room. Most warders are tall, strong and athletic in appearance and to the whimpering group of children on the point of being inhumanly caned, such executioners must look indeed frightening. No wonder the children whimper long before the first swirl of the cane is heard aloft.

The first child receives the first lash and he screams – but he is not to receive the balance of his due just yet – that is reserved and he is passed on to the back end of the queue. Another child is brought forward by strong arms and receives his first searing cut. He too, is passed on to the end of the queue. The 'Devil's Parade' goes on – each child sees each other one receive cuts with a stout cane inflicted on the bare skin of each of the other crying boys, most of them not yet in their teens. Those with the fewest cuts awarded by the magistrates are done first and they stand in a corner, still witnessing the torments of those who have not yet paid the full price for lapsing through hunger or some other tragic cause.

Ultimately the last cut has been inflicted on the child with the longest sentence and all are ejected from the jail, still weeping and chattering with fear. Let it not be thought that the cane comes down with a mild school-masterly swish. No: the wardens do not do things that way when dealing with their '*landsgenote*' (fellow-citizens) who happen to be darker. The jail official is invariably a powerful man and he bends to his task with manifest determination if not sadistic glee. When he lashes he lashes. Civilian observers who have witnessed this cruel performance are often too sickened to speak of what they have seen. They are haunted in their sleep and prefer not to confess that they have allowed themselves to be witnesses to such bestiality.

(C 8/8/59)

CHAPTER SEVEN

Strike Breaking and Crowd 'Control'
by the South African Police

The Pan-Africanist Congress of South Africa, an anti-apartheid movement, called on all Africans to hand their hated passes back to the authorities on March 21, 1960. The response to this call was greater than the response to any earlier call to defy apartheid. That day some ten thousand people collected, in a peaceful manner, round the police station at Sharpeville, near Vereeniging, Transvaal. Some of the young white police panicked, and started firing into the crowd. Sixty-nine peaceful demonstrators died, and over a hundred were injured.

There was also shooting and killing near Cape Town, at Langa, that same day.

Thereafter the government declared a state of emergency. The Pan-Africanist Congress called on the people of Cape Town, where I was living, to stay away from work. Again the response of the people was tremendous, and unprecedented. Virtually every African stayed in his home and refused to go to work. Cape Town's docks were immobilized, for the first time by strike action. The authorities felt that this silent, peaceful withdrawal of labour was a victory for the P.A.C. and decided to flog the people back to work.

On April 2, twelve days after Sharpeville, the governor-general, C. R. Swart, signed an amendment to the emergency regulations. This amendment read as follows:

3. (1) Whenever any magistrate or any commissioned or non-commissioned officer in the Forces is of opinion that the presence or conduct of any person or persons at any place endangers or may endanger the public safety or the maintenance of public order or exposes or may ex-

pose life or property to danger, he may in a loud voice order such person or persons to stop or to proceed to any place indicated in the order or to desist from such conduct, and shall thereupon warn such person or persons that force will be used if the order is not obeyed forthwith.

(2) If any such order is not obeyed forthwith, the magistrate or commissioned or non-commissioned officer may apply or authorize the application of force (including force resulting in death) in order to remove or prevent the suspected danger. . . .

In another place in the same order the definition of persons against whom force, including force resulting in death, may be used, is extended to include: a person 'who in any manner advises incites or encourages any other person to stay away from . . . his work . . . with intent to thwart or to exact concessions from the government or any other lawful authority or to cause general dislocation or to cripple or prejudice any industry or undertaking . . . *or to prejudice any person or to prejudice employers in general* . . . or with the said intent is absent from his work or refuses to undertake or perform any work'. (My emphasis.)

This order, typically, was made retrospective to April 1.

Thus the head of state, the cruel Swart as it happened, authorized any non-commissioned officer of the forces (and this included the police) to beat or kill anyone who stayed away from work. And on that day practically every African in and near Cape Town was away from work.

The police went into action on the fourth. The atmosphere of that day's repression is conveyed by a report I did for *Contact* at the time.

CAPE TOWN: At 9 a.m. on Monday, 4th April, I was a passenger in a taxi at the big central intersection of Darling

68

and Buitenkant Streets a few hundred yards from the Cape Town City Hall. The taxi stopped for traffic lights to turn green.

I noticed a good many white police, in uniform, standing at the intersection on the southern corner. Suddenly two of them started rushing across Darling Street to the corner near the Castle. I noticed a small group of African men – say, two or three – running for their lives away from these police who had just noticed them and were chasing them.

Before the chase began the African men had been walking quietly towards the City Hall on the pavement.

The police ran very fast, and easily caught them. They began beating them on the head, neck and shoulders with sticks. The sticks appeared to be about $2\frac{1}{2}$ or 3 feet long. One of the victims screamed.

There were many pedestrians and many cars at this busy intersection. The assault was done in front of them all.

Suddenly another policeman, on our side of Darling Street, began chasing another African whom he had seen. He had a heavy 3-ft. sjambok made from a motor car tyre. He chased the African past the front of our taxi. I put my head out and roared: 'Stop it, you swine', in a voice that reached several hundred yards.

The policeman did stop it, and came to me in a menacing and extremely angry spirit. He shouted at me and asked me if I knew there was a state of emergency, said I was obstructing the police, and threatened me with imprisonment. He was joined by a sergeant, who said much the same. I said to him, in a peremptory tone: 'Your men are behaving like swine. Call them off.'

At this the first policeman walked off cursing me in a selection of four-letter words.

I asked the sergeant to listen, and to stop his policemen from being obscene. A third policeman came up to me, and said: 'Ah, we know *you*,' and went away.

This was only one out of countless incidents in Cape

Town on that day. At Claremont I learned that the police collected a large group of Africans at the Police Station, and thrashed them in full view of the white, African, and coloured onlookers. Many telephoned the press, and swamped the incoming lines of the two big dailies.

Here are some of their stories:

An African nurse called friends outside to beg for supplies of bandages and antiseptic. Her first aid station had run out as injured flooded in.

'Police are beating up everybody,' she sobbed over the telephone when I called her. 'Blood is everywhere.'

White Capetonians too began to complain angrily. As the morning wore on – it seems that the 'operation' on the townships began before dawn – police parties began tumbling from riot trucks and beating up Africans in the city's suburbs.

'I can't stand the screaming,' telephoned an Englishman from Maitland, a middle-class suburb. He reported seeing policemen slashing at Africans with sjamboks right outside the police station.

Eye-witnesses agreed that in many cases there was no doubt that entirely innocent and often elderly Africans were struck by khaki-clad youngsters, who had obviously been told to get tough and not to worry about the consequences.

A local newspaper reporter, Douglas Alexander, was arrested for trying to take pictures of incidents in another white area. He was later released with a caution.

In a statement on the evening of the 5th, minister of justice Erasmus said that allegations that members of the South African Police were using undue force in dealing with African intimidators were unsubstantiated.

But Colonel I. P. S. Terblanche, deputy-commissioner of police, Cape Western Area, said in a statement: 'Under the new regulations Natives who cannot account for themselves where they might cause trouble can be dealt with on the spot. They are being dealt with. Our aim is not to make arrests but to deal with trouble-makers on the spot.'

(C 16/4/60)

Many were killed. The hospitals were full of the injured. Members of the Liberal Party, showing no fear, went round the hospitals collecting affidavits and statements.

The police did not content themselves with beating people in the streets. They went through the houses in Nyanga and Langa. This is what happened to one of the householders:

> Hammington Majija lives with his family at Nyanga and, until recently, worked for a picture-framing firm in Woodstock.
>
> Today he is out of work and has a fractured left arm and a fractured thumb on his right hand. He is behind on instalments for the hire-purchase furniture in his Nyanga home.
>
> This is the story he told me today: 'On Thursday last week – the day of the big police drive – I was at home with my wife. I sent my children to Stellenbosch.
>
> 'On Thursday afternoon I heard the helicopter overhead – it was telling people to stay in their homes.
>
> 'Then I heard a knock on the back door. I went to the door and found some police and soldiers there. A policeman raised some sort of club and struck me. They chased me into the bedroom. I raised my arms to ward off the policeman's blows and was struck several times on the arms.
>
> 'They chased me outside and I fell to the ground. Someone struck me on the back.
>
> 'The next day I saw a doctor and he sent me to hospital to be X-rayed. At hospital they put my right thumb and my left arm in plaster.
>
> 'On Friday morning I went to work and my employer said I had stayed away from work and he was sacking me. My wife, who works as a domestic servant in my employer's home, has also been sacked. (C 7/5/60)

71

The Pretoria Bus Boycott Meeting

In January 1957 there was a bus boycott in Lady Selborne, then Pretoria's biggest African township. The boycott began just after new year. Many people turned to the railway service, and to cope with the increased number of passengers the railway administration increased the number of trains, and the number of coaches on the trains. In this way the people were able to avoid using the bus service, which was completely boycotted, except by some employees of the bus company.

The government decided to use intimidation. The first act, on January 28, was that all the extra trains and coaches were taken off. The railway refused to sell daily tickets or single tickets to the people, and the only people accepted as passengers were those with old-standing season tickets. New season tickets were refused on January 28. The minister of transport, one of the less uncivilized of the ministers of the South African government, Ben J. Schoeman, said: 'The extra train services have been discontinued because if the people want to get to work they must use the buses'. Thus the majesty of the central government was thrown in on the side of the bus company, and against the people's boycott.

The people reacted well. That evening a meeting was called in Lady Selborne. By 7 p.m. there were about a thousand people at the meeting, which was orderly at every stage. As the crowd swelled, the fears of the authorities clearly grew, and they sent along a force of police, armed with many weapons including sten light automatic guns.

'Then the African leaders were told by the police to send the people home. At the same time the police left the trucks and lined up beside them. Most were armed with long batons or knobkerries, but a number carried sten guns and the Europeans were also armed with revolvers.' (Then the people began to disperse.) 'Some were singing *Nkosi sikelel' i-Afrika* (national hymn of the African people). Then the police charged, laying about them with their batons and knobkerries. Men and women were felled to the ground, and a pistol shot rang out.' A man was later admitted to the Pretoria General Hospital with a serious bullet wound in the head. (CT 29/1/57)

Other incidents

In June 1957 some seventy torch-bearing young people of Indian origin, peacefully leading a march to celebrate the Congress Movement's 'day of protest', were dispersed by 60 white and non-white police. (A 27/6/57)

At the opening of the treason trial against 152 persons in December 1956, elements in the crowd outside the court booed the police. The police were armed with sten guns. They used them. Twenty-two people were taken to hospital as a result. (O 20/12/56)

CHAPTER EIGHT

The Recklessness of the Violence

In South Africa if you are black and 'cheeky' you can be shot dead by an officer of the law. Not lawfully, of course, but it does happen. It happened to an African named Alfred Stephens, who died on November 2, 1956.

The policeman, a white man named Willem Gideon Johannes Spence, aged 19, was asked what had happened after he shot Alfred Stephens. He replied to the questioner, a white woman, 'I threatened to shoot him and he said "shoot then". So I shot him. He was cheeky'. (RDM 16/8/57)

If you are black, in South Africa, and are a cyclist, you can be assaulted just because you are black and a cyclist. This happened in a case in which two policemen, Andries Janse van Rensburg, aged 23, and another, unnamed, aged 18, were charged. The evidence in their case showed that they had driven along in their car, flogging African cyclists in the face as they passed them with a heavy sjambok (rhino hide whip).

They also hit a white man on a cycle, Petrus Johannes Pieterson. He said he was cycling towards Vereeniging, Transvaal, when a man in a passing car hit him in the face with a sjambok. He felt a searing pain. Questioned by police, Van Rensburg said he had hit Pieterson 'because he thought he was a Native'. One of the Africans who was hit said that the blow on his left temple was so hard that it flung him off his bicycle. (CT 8/1/59)

Using the safety of one's motor car to assault Africans is a sport that is taught young, in South Africa. A Johannesburg couple, out for their Sunday afternoon drive in their car, saw a big stone land in an African fruit-seller's basket. Frightened, the fruit-seller ran away, nearly knocking over his basket. The couple then saw that in a car in front of them with the registration letters TA (Benoni) a white boy was leaning out of the window waving his hands and shrieking with delight. A little further on he aimed a stone at another fruit-seller, and just missed him. 'Apparently determined not to miss again, the boy leant right out of the car when he saw two Africans on bicycles. Almost able to touch one of them, he took careful aim and hurled a fist-sized stone between the shoulder-blades of one of the cyclists. It nearly knocked him off his bicycle. He swerved and a Johannesburg car behind swerved to miss him, and narrowly missed a serious accident.' The driver of the Benoni car, a woman, clearly approved of what the boy was doing. The couple who witnessed this said that they 'had read about such incidents, but this was the first time they had actually seen one'. (S 12/2/58)

Recklessness, too, I see in the use of acid by the police in their assaults on prisoners in their care. In July 1961 Sergeant Johan Groesbeek Mare was alleged to have assaulted a prisoner, Robert Vilagazi, by beating him with a belt, and by pouring acid on his head. It is true that perjury entered into this case, but the fact remains that a policeman made a sworn statement saying that Mare had done this. So even if this fearful story were not true (which it probably is), the fact remains that gruesome ideas such as this exist in the minds of the South African Police.

Reckless, too, was the killing of Jantjie Masangu. He was listening to a juke-box in a tea-room when a police van stopped outside on September 24, 1961, a Sunday afternoon. Naturally he ran away. He ran about 1,000 yards down to a dam, chased by a white constable. He jumped into the dam and disappeared. A white eye-witness gave this statement to the press: 'The Native jumped into the water there. While the European policeman stood on the bank, the Native came up three times – calling for help. The policeman shouted to my father, who

was sitting over there: "Go in and get him out. I can't swim."
My father replied: "I can't swim either." We saw him drown
and disappear. I was present when the police fished his body
out next morning. His arms were still above his head as they
were when he disappeared for the last time".

The district commandant of police was questioned about
this case. He told the press that his information was that the
police believed Masangu had hidden in the reeds round the
dam. They believed that he had escaped when they could not
find him on their second visit.

But, when the press man looked for reeds at the dam, he
saw that there were no reeds at all at that dam. (ST 29/10/31)

Do not, if you are black, and if you value your life, try to
escape from the South African police. The whites are all armed.
And there is a state of undeclared war between the tribes in
South Africa. It is like a British soldier trying to escape from
his German captors at the time of Dunkirk. You get shot. This
happened at East London, Cape, on about October 10, 1959,
when a young policeman fired three shots in quick succession
at a range of about ten yards in a crowded street at an escaping
prisoner, and killed him.

No attempt was made to call on the public to stop the prisoner. He had just been convicted on a trivial offence, and had
been sentenced to a fine of £5 or 20 days' imprisonment. But
he made the mistake of running. The killer's name was not
reported, but the police chiefs promised 'a departmental inquiry'.

Finally, if you are black, and you value your life, do not
criticize the police. And when the police strike at a man to
defend their good reputation, do not try to intervene, if you
are black. For this is how a West Indian sailor, Milton King,
lost his life in Durban, in 1951.

Witnesses told the court how two white policemen, on patrol

76

in Dock Road, Durban, heard singing in a pub. They went in, and stood listening to the singing of five coloured men. One of the men pointed to the police and said to King: 'These are the real Boers'. One of the policemen, Johannes S. K. Visser, kicked this man's chair from under him. He then put him back on the chair. King, the West Indian, said to the policeman 'What did you do that for?' The policeman knocked King down twice. 'I wanted him out of action in order that I could arrest him for using obscene language', said Visser. On the way to the charge office King said: 'The London police would not have arrested me. They would have warned me'. The other policeman, constable Jacobus Johannes Groenewald, said: 'I want to hit you'. He hit King, who fell on the pavement. Groenewald felt King's head, and said he was 'lights out'. The two then carried the man, whose head was 'soft', to the police station, and laid a charge against him for 'drunkenness'. King died shortly afterwards. (S 14/6/51)

Another example of recklessness in violence and the threat of violence occurred in about 1956. The Sunnyside poultry farm at Grasmere, near Evaton, Transvaal, erected a large notice, some twelve feet high, next to its fence which bordered the national road from Johannesburg to Vanderbijlpark. This notice read:

DANGER (skull and crossbones sign)

NATIVES, INDIANS AND COLOUREDS
If you enter these premises at night you will be listed as missing. Armed guards shoot on sight. Savage dogs devour the corpse. You have been warned.

Tens of thousands of Africans and other non-whites saw this notice daily, as it was on the main route from the populous suburb of Evaton to Johannesburg.

The notice was publicized. One day, as I was passing, I went in to ask the owner to pull it down. I found a manager, as the proprietor was away near Pietermaritzburg on another poultry farm that he owned. The manager said he would tell the owner that he had had a protest.

The matter was raised in parliament, where the minister of justice, C. R. Swart, said that he would take no action to have the notice removed. But soon afterwards the notice was removed.

Interestingly, some months later it was replaced. But a few nights later it was forcibly torn down. So far as I know it has never been replaced since then.

CHAPTER NINE

Violence in Jail

The South African Police do not control the prisons. Prisons are under the control of a separate department, the prisons department. But the sort of men recruited for the prisons are similar to the men recruited for the police force. They have a similar khaki uniform. They treat the non-whites in their charge much as the police do.

The first major exposé of the prison scandal in South Africa was made by *Drum*, a courageous monthly owned by Jim Bailey, and edited at that time by Anthony Sampson, a journalist and author with an international reputation.

By brilliant pressmanship, *Drum* got photographs of the inside of the Fort, Johannesburg's and South Africa's biggest prison, from the high roof of a nearby hospital. Some of these photographs showed the humiliations of the 'tausa' dance. It is a dance conducted under the pretence of searching the prisoners when they return from work outside the prison. The regulations say that prisoners must be searched 'with due regard to decency and self-respect, and in as seemly a manner as consistent with the necessity of discovering any concealed article on or in any part of his body or clothing'. (Regulation 388(b) of the prisons regulations, 1911.)

Prisoners, but only non-white prisoners, are made to strip naked when they return to jail. Then they are made to jump up in the air, clapping their hands, opening their mouths, then turning round. This is known as 'tausa' or 'the Zulu dance'.

Drum published its remarkable photographs, and commented: '*Drum* submits that the method of searching shown in these two photographs has no regard whatever to decency or self-respect; that it is neither necessary or even effective in preventing smuggling; and that it should be stopped forthwith'.

Drum also got a journalist into jail. One of its staffers, brave Henry Nxumalo, whom I and many others knew well, and who is now dead, got himself convicted. His story is best told in his own words. It should be mentioned that most South African prisons operate on an unofficial agreement between certain long-term non-white prisoners and the authorities. In exchange for certain privileges these prisoners rule their fellow-prisoners and exploit them cruelly. This is part of Henry Nxumalo's story:

> I served five days' imprisonment at the Johannesburg Central Prison from January 20 to January 24. My crime was being found without a night pass five minutes before midnight, and I was charged under the curfew regulations. I was sentenced to a fine of 10s or five days' imprisonment.
>
> Two constables arrested me at the corner of Rissik and Plein Streets. I was taken to Marshall Square Police Station, charged, searched, given two blankets and locked up in the cells together with 37 others. The night was long. The prison doors kept clanging as more prisoners trickled in during the night. The cell itself was dark. I couldn't tell the day from the night. Only the familiar shout of the young constable carrying a noisy bunch of prison keys told us it was morning.
>
> We had roll-call, breakfast, got back our personal effects and were packed like sardines – over 40 of us – in a truck and delivered to the cells below the magistrate's court. When we got off the truck into the cells below the courts, one elderly-looking prisoner was a little slow to climb off. The prisoners were jostling to get off at once and blocking the way and when the old man reached the ground he nearly missed the direction the other prisoners were taking. He looked about and S saw him. He hit him with his open hand on the temples and told him to wake up.
>
> Before we appeared in court I asked one of the black

80

5. Perhaps the most dramatic photograph to come out of to-day's turmoil in South Africa. The need to search returning prisoners has become a daily occasion to humiliate the African prisoners by making them do the 'tausa' dance. This photograph, of the interior of the Fort, Johannesburg's main prison, was taken by a Drum photographer from the high roof of a neighbouring hospital with a telephoto lens. See p. 79.

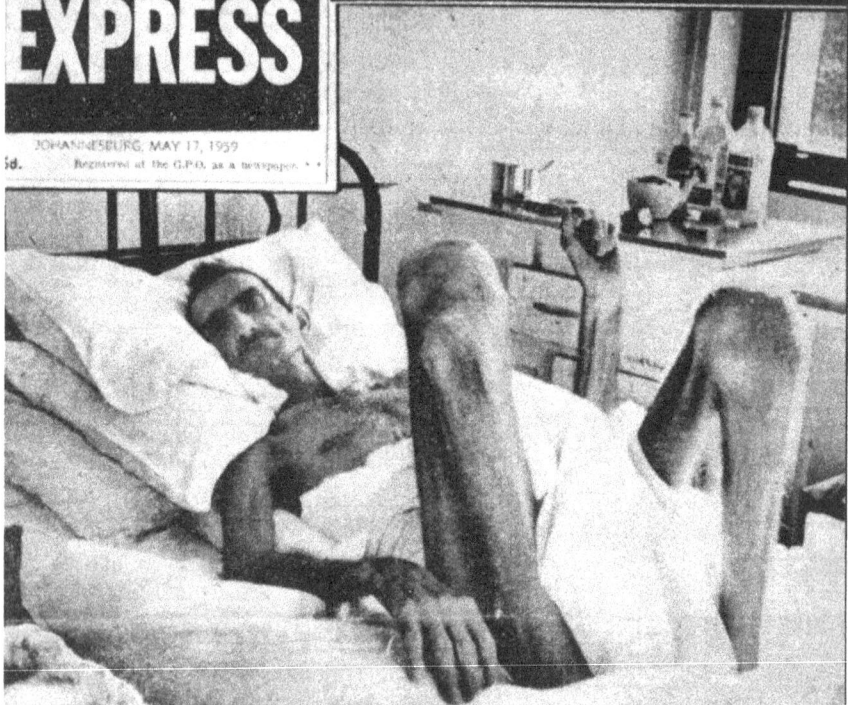

SUNDAY EXPRESS

THIS PICTURE WILL SHOCK YO...

JOHANNESBURG, MAY 17, 1959

5d. Registered at the G.P.O. as a newspaper

6. Occasionally this police violence turns against white people. Here is a photograph of a man, T. D. van Schalkwyk, who was jumped on by a young policeman while he was incapably drunk, and whose weight dropped from 200 lbs to under 90 lbs before he died. See p. 90.

constables to allow me to phone my employers and my family. He said: 'Go on, voetsek!' Meanwhile white prisoners in the opposite cells were phoning their families and their employers without trouble from a wall telephone near the warder.

After our cases had been heard by the magistrate, we were sent back to the cells. Convicted prisoners who couldn't raise enough money to pay their fines employed various methods to get money. They either borrowed from those who had much less or bartered their clothes, promising to release their benefactors as soon as they were out. Discharged prisoners took messages to relatives of convicted prisoners.

This lasted about two hours; we were checked and taken to Johannesburg Central Prison by truck. We arrived at the prison immediately after one o'clock. From the truck we were given orders to 'shayisa' (close up), fall in twos and 'sharp shoot' (run) to the prison reception office. From then on 'Come on, Kaffir' was the operative phrase from both black and white prison officials, and in all languages.

Many of us who were going to prison for the first time didn't know exactly where the reception office was. Although the prison officials were with us, no one was directing us. But if a prisoner hesitated, slackened his half-running pace and looked round, he got a hard boot kick on the buttocks, a slap on his face or a whipping from the warders. Fortunately there were some second offenders with us who knew where to go. We followed them through the prison's many zig-zagging corridors until we reached the reception office.

The reception office had a terrifyingly brutal atmosphere. It was full of foul language. A number of khaki-uniformed white officials stood behind a long cement bar-like curved counter. They wore the initials 'PSGD' on their shoulders. When they were not joking about prisoners, they were swearing at them and taking down their particulars. Two were taking fingerprints and hitting the prisoners in the face when they made mistakes.

Five long-term prisoners attended to us. One came up to me and said he knew me. I didn't know him. He asked for cigarettes, but I didn't have any. Another told us to take off our watches and money and hold them in our hands.

'That's a fine pen you've got, eh?' he asked. 'How about giving it to me?' I said :'I'm afraid I can't; it's not my pen, it's my boss's pen.' 'Hi, don't tell me lies, you bastard,' he said, 'what the hell are you doing with your boss's pen in prison? Did you steal it?' he asked. I said I hadn't stolen it. I was using it and had it in my possession when I was arrested. 'Give it here, I want it for my work here; if you refuse you'll see blood streaming down your dirty mouth soon!' I was nervous, but didn't reply. 'Look, you little fool, I'll see that you are well treated in prison if you give me that pen.' The other prisoners looked at me anxiously. I didn't know whether they approved of my giving my pen or not; but their anxious look seemed to suggest that their fate in prison lay in that pen. I gave it away.

From there I ran down to the end of the wide curved desk to have my height taken, and stood beside the measuring rod, naked. The long-term prisoner taking my height asked for my name and checked it against my ticket.

When finished with a prisoner, he would *throw his ticket on the floor for the prisoner to pick it up* and get on with the next one.

Then our prison clothes were thrown at us – a red shirt and a torn white pair of short pants. They looked clean; but the side cap and the white jacket which were issued to me later were filthy. The jacket had dry sweat on the neck.

Some said the clothes they were wearing had been worn by the prisoners detained for V.D.

After another roll-call we were marched to the top of the court to collect our food. The dishes were lined in rows and each prisoner picked up the dish nearest to him. The zinc dishes containing the food were rusty. The top of my dish was broken in three places. The food itself was boiled whole mealies with fat. We were marched to No 7 cell, given blankets and a sleeping mat and locked in. We ate. The time was about 4.30 p.m. Clean water and toilet buckets were installed. But that water wasn't enough for 60 people. The long-term prisoners warned us not to use the water as if we were at our own homes. An old man went to fetch water with his dish at one stage and the long-term prisoner in charge of the cell swore at him. The old man insisted that he was thirsty and continued scooping the water. The long-term prisoner took the water away from him and threw it all over the old man's face.

There was a stinking smell when prisoners used the toilet bucket at night without toilet paper. At 8 p.m. the bell rang and we were ordered to be quiet and sleep. Some prisoners who had smuggled dagga and matches into the cell started conversing in whispers and smoking. The blankets were full of bugs; I turned round and round during the night without being able to sleep, and kept my prison clothes on for protection against bugs.

We were up at about six o'clock the following morning. I tried to get some water to wash my dish and drink. The dish was full of the previous night's fat, and I didn't know how I was going to do it. But the long-term prisoner shouted at me and ordered me to leave the water alone. I obeyed. He swore at me in Afrikaans, and ordered me to wipe the urine which was overflowing from the toilet bucket with a small sack cloth. I did so. He said I must wipe it dry; but the cloth was so small that the floor remained wet.

He told me to find two other prisoners to help me carry the toilet bucket out, empty it and clean it. It was full of the night's excrement. There were no volunteers. so I slipped to a corner and waited. He saw me and rushed at me. 'What did I tell you, damn it; what did I say?' He slapped me on my left cheek with his right open hand as he spoke. He said he could have me put in solitary confinement if he wished. He could tell the chief warder that I had messed the floor and I would get an additional punishment. I kept quiet. I had done nothing of the sort. Finally he ordered two other prisoners to help me.

In the four days I was in prison – I got a remission of one day – I was kicked or thrashed every day. I saw many other prisoners being thrashed daily. I was never told what was expected of me, but had to guess. Sometimes I guessed wrong and got into trouble.

Long-term and short-term prisoners mixed freely at the prison. For example the famous A—— D——, of Alexandra Township, who is doing a 10-year sentence for various crimes, was one of the most important persons in prison during my time. He was responsible for the in and out movements of other prisoners and respected by prisoners and warders. Though I was a short-term prisoner, I, too, took orders from A——.

It was a common practice for short-term prisoners to give their small piece of meat to long-term prisoners on meat days for small favours such as tobacco, dagga, shoes (which are supposed to be supplied to coloured prisoners only), wooden spoons – or to ensure that they were always supplied with sleeping mats.

Many other prisoners shared the same fate. There are no directions or rules read or posted in prison. At least I didn't see any. Thrashing time for warders was roll-call and break-fast time as well as supper time. For long-term prisoners it was inside the cells at all times. Long-term prisoners thrash-ed more prisoners more severely and much oftener than the prison officials themselves, and often in the presence of either white or black warders.

On the day of our discharge we were mustered in a big hall at breakfast and checked. There was an open lavatory at the corner of the hall. Six men used it, and when the seventh one went a long-term prisoner swore at him and told him to keep his stomach full until he reached home. He said the man belonged to a tribe he detested: a tribe which killed his brother.

We were then marched to the Reception Office for our personal effects and checking out. The long-term prisoners officiating there told us not to think that we were already out of prison. They kicked and slapped prisoners for the slightest mistake, and sometimes for no mistake at all; and promised them additional sentences if they complained. In the office there was a notice warning prisoners to see that their personal belongings were recorded in the prison's books correctly and exactly as they had brought them. But I dared not complain about my pen which was commandeered on my arrival, lest I be detained. Even the prisoner who took it pretended not to know me.

Before we left prison we were told the Superintendent would address us. We could make complaints to him if we had any. But the fat Zulu warder who paraded us to the yard for the Superintendent's inspection said we must tell him everything was all right if we want to leave prison. 'This is a court of law,' he said; 'you are about to go home, but before you leave this prison the big boss of the prison will address you. He will ask you if you have any complaints. Now I take it that you all want to go to your homes – to your wives and children – you don't want to stay here. So if the big boss asks you if everything is all right say, 'Yes, Sir.' If he says have you any complaints say, 'No, Sir.' You hear?'

In a chorus we said 'Yes.'

One by one we zigzagged our way out of the prison's many doors and gates and lined up in two's in front of the main and final gate. We were ordered to leave prison quietly and in pairs when the small gate was open. If we blocked the gate we would be thrashed. We were to come out in the order of the line. The man on the left would go out first and the one on the right would follow. The gate was opened. We saw freedom and blocked the gate in our anxiety. If they thrashed us we couldn't feel it . . . we didn't look back!

Sometimes white South Africa uses its power to jail people to impose its will in civil disputes. Take the case of Johannes Mahlangu, an independent builder who was maimed when he had a dispute with a white farmer with whom he had a contract. The terms of the contract throw light on the terrible economic weakness under which the non-white people of South Africa labour. Here is the story, as told by a *Sunday Times* (Johannesburg) reporter:

> Johannes Mahlangu, a labourer with a family, entered into a contract with a white farmer six miles from his home.
> For £22 he undertook to:
>> Build and roof three rooms of 222 square feet in area.
>> Do other major reconstruction jobs and plaster inside and outside.
>> Pay his own assistants, 'eat his own food, work every day early and late, supply and transport at his own cost all sand, stone and concrete to complete the work.'
> He was paid £11 during the course of the work.
> When he went to collect the remaining £11 he and a companion were accused of stealing two fowls. They were taken to jail.
> Three weeks later, Mahlangu – unable to walk – was helped into court. His attorney, drawing attention to his condition, said 'There must be something seriously wrong at the jail for a man who entered it in perfect health now to be unable to walk and clearly urgently in need of medical attention.'
> The magistrate instructed the prosecutor to call for an explanation from the chief warder.
> This week the magistrate told me he was satisfied with

the chief warder's explanation. He was 'generally known as a good man.' He believed Mahlangu was not injured in the prison but in a farm accident.

Mahlangu, whom I saw on the farm on which he lives with his family, is still unable to walk.

He says that three days after his admission to jail he and the man arrested with him, were assaulted by an indeterminate sentence prisoner who acts as a kind of 'induna' – or headman – in the jail.

Mahlangu says that, unable to walk, he was left lying around in the prison without medical attention. He was then assisted into court and released with a suspended sentence.

His white employers confirm that he was in a perfect state of health when he was arrested.

(ST 29/10/61)

The Mahlangu case is another case in which is demonstrated the fearful power delegated by the prison authorities to the African long-term prisoners.

Another interesting facet of the Mahlangu case is that the prison concerned was the prison at Middelburg, Transvaal, in the heart of the notorious potato country of east Transvaal, in which farm labourers are treated more shamefully than in any other part of South Africa.

Another case in which the long-term prisoners inflicted serious injuries on a man was the case of Ernest Edward Groenewald, a contractor of Heathfield, Cape Town. Though his tax payments were in order, there was a misunderstanding over his tax receipts and he was jailed in Roeland Street prison, Cape Town. In the cells, that night, some demands were made on him by the long-term men. He refused. They assaulted him. The prison superintendent, Lieut L. F. Bottcher, confirmed that Groenewald had been 'seriously injured'. Charges were

87

laid against seven prisoners. Bottcher somewhat self-righteously added that 'we are doing out utmost to prevent these dirty attacks, but we simply cannot control them'. Officials admitted that such attacks were a daily occurrence. (CT 3/11/60)

I can myself testify how little reliance can be placed on Bottcher's word. For I myself witnessed a small assault in his prison while I was a prisoner there in 1960. The victim was a coloured man: the assailant was a white warder named Mostert. As Mostert hit him:

> the man cringed, obviously used to being pushed around. It was not a serious assault. But I was a magistrate for twelve years and I know an assault when I see one. It was a rough push and a slight blow, and it was done in a bullying manner.
>
> I reported the assault to the Chief Warder, Warder Payne. He asked me to submit a report in writing which I did. He called in the prisoner, and the warder, and after listening to the three of us he said to me: 'I will see that he (meaning the warder) gets a choke-off.'
>
> The next day I was summoned into the office of the officer commanding, Lieut Bottcher. He was with Chief Warder Payne. On his desk lay the report I had made, with other pieces of paper attached to it.
>
> He said to me in a domineering tone: 'Duncan, I haven't read this (pointing to my report). But I know what is in it.' He then said that he realised that I had gone round his prison trying to 'see things'. I denied this, but said that I had in fact seen what I had reported. He told me that it was none of my business, and warned me to 'keep my eyes shut' in future. (C 19/11/60)

I had earlier been allowed some privileges in that prison, notably a chair and table, and a second felt mat. These were all taken from me, leaving me to sleep on the wooden floor with nothing but one felt mat and three blankets. I have no doubt that this was punishment for the report I made.

When I read of the authorities boasting of how keen they are to stop brutality I often think of this otherwise insignificant happening in my life.

CHAPTER TEN

Last Word on the Police

Here are a few unsorted facts about the violence used by the police.

Of course, most of the violence is used to maintain apartheid, and against the non-whites. But if you brutalize a white policeman you cannot always guarantee that his brutality will not sometimes hurt white victims. One of these was T. D. van Schalkwyk, of Vanderbijlpark, Transvaal. He was picked up drunk by constable Jan Gerhardus Terblanche on February 6, 1959. He was taken, very drunk, by Terblanche and another person to the police station. A witness said that he 'heard a kind of thud as though somebody had been struck. I went back to where we had left Van Schalkwyk and saw Terblanche jump on his stomach twice with his boots on. . . . He was lying flat on his back when Terblanche jumped on him. I pulled Terblanche off and told him that he had already done enough damage. He was very angry'. The witness and Terblanche bathed Van Schalkwyk's face and tried to revive him – but failed. Terblanche washed away marks made by his boots on Van Schalkwyk's stomach.

What happened was that Van Schalkwyk lost a great deal of blood through internal bleeding, and had 24 pints of blood given to him by transfusions.

Van Schalkwyk lived after that assault for about three and a half months, in hospital. He lost weight constantly. In health he had weighed 200 poounds, but before his death he weighed no more than 90 pounds. He died on May 18. Just before he died his wife gave birth to their ninth child, but he was too weak to be told this.

And there is one case in my records in which a white man got the electrical torture treatment: the case of Eugene Maree of Erfdeel farm, Odendaalsrus, Orange Free State. The police suspected that he and some Africans had possession of stolen property, so they hit him over the ear, hit his head against the wall, and inflicted electrical assaults on him by tying one wire to his ear and one to one of his fingers. His mother, Mrs Hendriet Lorraine Maree, got off with a throttling, being kicked on the buttocks, having her arm twisted, and being hit with a cane. Two months passed before she would tell the doctor what the police had done to her, as she was 'in an anxiety state' and 'mentally and physically shocked' and believed, mistakenly, that the police were always eavesdropping and listening while she was talking to the doctor. She told the doctor that she was afraid of being sent back to the cells. Her 'anxiety state' continued for several more months. (CT 6, 8/9/61)

This willingness to use torture on a fellow-Afrikaner white bodes ill for those white democrats who are caught while resisting apartheid, especially those held for questioning under the 90-day clause.

Enough has been said to show how cruel are the policemen who are the first defence of the apartheid system. The final word must remain with a letter-writer to the Cape nationalist daily *Die Burger*. He clearly did not think that the police were tough enough: 'We must look squarely at the facts, and we must take care that the police must no longer be used as a football by the criminal. These things have now gone too far, and we, the public, are tired of the way in which our police are defied. I often wonder if our nation has not become too democratic, and whether we should not use the sjambok more and talk less'. (27/6/58)

CHAPTER ELEVEN

The Worst Farm Labour System in the World

The above heading is a wide generalization, yet I believe that it is no more than the sober truth. In other lands, admittedly, peasants are treated harshly, and are forced to work sometimes against their will. In China in some of the communes men and women are harnassed to ploughs, and communist guards stand over them with rifles. In Latin America powerful landlords exploit their serf-like servants. South Africa seems to combine the worst features of all other known systems. And the basic reason is that one tribe, which hates and fears another, is in a position of unquestioned power over that other tribe.

Let us take a cruel landlord in, say Latin America. What restrains him from hurting and killing the relatively powerless people under him? Surely, apart from the sometimes questionable efficacity of the law, two factors operate to protect the weak. The first is that, in all but a few areas there are ties of blood and nationality that connect master and serf. And the second is that the legal system is weak enough to allow a monstrously tyrannical master to be killed in revenge by the families under him. In South Africa there are no ties of kinship or nationality between master and man. In South Africa the police network covers the whole country effectively. And in South Africa the master is armed to the teeth, while the men are disarmed.

For these reasons, although some masters treat their men kindly in South Africa, there is a universal injustice, an unfairness in the sharing of rewards. There is a lack of personal freedom of movement. There is poverty and ignorance on a vast scale. And there are cruelties which in other countries would seem incredible.

True, some cases get into court. And some courts have visited proper punishment on the killers and torturers that are sentenced. But one investigator gave as his opinion that for every case that goes before the courts, about three go unreported. (P 11/12/55)

In this report, concrete cases of cruelties will be first recorded. Then the legal and social background of the South African farming system will be briefly described.

'Mpikwa crawled about on all fours, trying to work . . .'
Johan Snyman, aged 50, and Matthys Snyman, aged 29, father and son, of Harmonie Farm, Koster district, Transvaal, together with three of their African labourers, tortured and killed Elias Mpikwa, aged 50, on their farm in 1954.

Mpikwa was a convict. He had likely been found away from his home without a pass, and had been sentenced to a term in prison. He had probably been moved into the Koster district because the farmers there needed more labour. He was in the absolute power of the Snymans.

Snyman (senior) told a witness that Mpikwa did not want to work so he flogged him. Another witness told how Snyman (junior), who was in charge of a party in the lands, kicked Mpikwa several times, telling him to 'work faster'.

The following morning Mpikwa told his friends, other prisoners, that his back was sore where he had been kicked the previous day. The prisoners were taken to the lands again – this was March 31, 1954 – and they were all naked, except for jute sacks draped around them. During the morning Snyman hit Mpikwa with a knobkerrie (stick with a heavy round knob at one end used as a club) because he was not working fast enough.

Snyman hit Mpikwa until he could not stand. While he was lying on the ground a young boy called Thlome came up and kicked him on the head and hit him. Thlome and another

African then picked Mpikwa up and threw him on to a truck. Snyman (senior) then arrived. Mpikwa was thrown off the truck. Snyman (senior) had a length of garden hose with him. Mpikwa began to work, but when he did Snyman (senior) hit him with the hose many times. Mpikwa then begged for water, and he was given a drink. Snyman (senior) then told his son that Mpikwa was not feeling the blows, so he doubled the hose-pipe. When he became tired he handed the double hosepipe to his son who continued hitting Mpikwa. When Snyman and his son had their afternoon tea they gave the hose to an African worker, Makgadi, saying 'he must hit'. Thlome then returned, took Mpikwa by the arm, and told him to stand up.

At one stage a labourer held up Mpikwa's leg so that Snyman (senior) could hit him between the legs.

Snyman then thrashed Mpikwa, who staggered slowly into the lands, then fell on his back. He roused himself and crawled about on all fours, trying to work.

Thlome and another African pleaded with Snyman to leave Mpikwa, but he was thrashed again. By this time he could not work, and Snyman ordered him into the truck. On the way back to the farmhouse Mpikwa became wide-eyed and his head sagged against the side of the truck.

Mpikwa died some time that afternoon. (S 29, 30/4/54)

'The baas threaded wire through a hole in my nose'
A case in which an African labourer fought back and killed his master occurred in the far west of the Cape Province, Barkly West, in 1952.

In this case Mack Thabong, aged 26, was charged with the murder of his employer, Frans Lock. What led up to the killing was described in court. Thabong was working for Lock, but wanted to go to a former employer at Andalusia. Lock said that if Thabong left he would kill him. Thabong started to walk away. Lock called him back and tied a thong round his waist and tied his hands together with wire. He then pierced the membrane between his nostrils and threaded wire through the hole, tied a thong to the wire, told him to pick up a shovel and led him to a place where there were two graves.

Lock ordered Thabong to dig up one of the graves. He did so. His wrists had been loosened but the wire was still through his nose. He could not dig deep into the grave because there were stones.

Lock again tied Thabong's hands with wire and led him to a dam. About five yards from the dam his baas said he must pray to God and say he was coming. When he had finished he would shoot him. His baas had a double-barrelled gun.

Thabong told the court what had happened.

'I said: Jesus help me, I am coming, Amen. As I said "amen" I hit the baas behind the ear with the spade. He fell to the ground and I took the gun. I tied his hands and feet with the wire in order that he would not follow me. I went to the outpost where I had been working and took the wire from my nostrils. I pushed the baas's bicycle to the house.'

Mrs Lock was sitting on the veranda with a gun near her on a chair. She asked him where the baas was. Thabong told her that he had hit him. Mrs Lock got up and picked up the gun. He sprang at her and took the gun away from her. She went into the bedroom and took something from beneath a pillow. (This was probably a pistol: there are probably pistols beneath pillows in a majority of white South African farmhouses.) As she came out of the bedroom he threw an iron bar at her that he had taken from the stove. He hit her twice more and she fell down. (S 22/3/52)

Here we have the thread that runs through so much of this violence: the gruesome embroidery on the fear of death. Tell God that you are coming. Dig a grave. This story of Thabong, ending in death for a farmer and a terrifying experience for his widow exemplifies the suffering that apartheid inflicts on the whites. They too are psychologically twisted by this inhuman system. Even when the white assailant comes out of the fight as physical victor, as he does nearly always, he comes out a spiritual cripple. And he, this spiritual cripple, is the dominant voice in South African politics. Verwoerd is his spokesman.

The one hope for the future, for white and black and for the country as a whole, is that the power to cripple themselves and cripple the Africans shall be firmly removed from such people. For one of the unarguable facts of the twentieth century is that such people have proved themselves unfitted to rule.

A dialogue from a South African farm
Mr. A. Harris, of the farm Overvloed, Babanango district, Natal had an altercation with one of his labourers, Mpikayise Majosi. Something had gone wrong in the work and the following exchange of words occurred:
Harris: 'All kaffirs ought to be killed.'
Majosi: 'All whites ought to be killed, especially the Boers. If all the whites were killed it would not be necessary for mangers to be built for the cattle, as there would be enough forage for everyone.'

After a tussle another farmer shot Majosi in the arm and was sentenced to a fine of £50 or four months in prison. (B 5/4/62)

Killing a baby
John Charles Holland, a farmer of the Seaforth area of the Philippolis district, deliberately ran down a group of Africans with his car on the Norvalspont-Philippolis bridge on the night of July 20, 1956, and killed a seven-month-old baby.

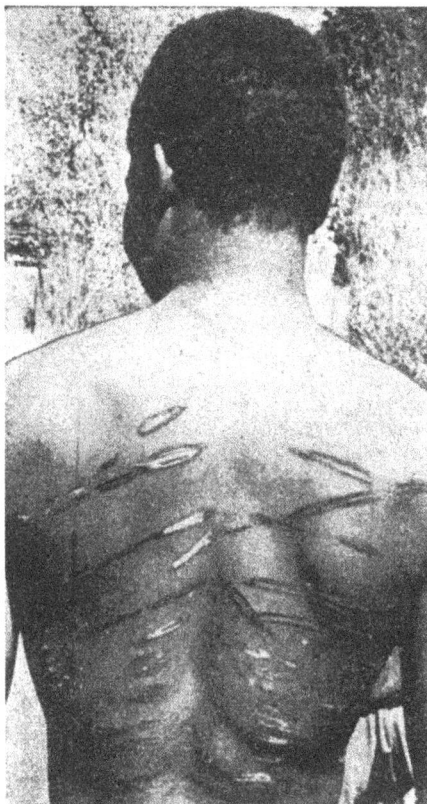

7. Typical of many hundreds, if not thousands of farm labourers, is John Gwala, who gave evidence in Heildelberg (Transvaal) against nine people charged with assaulting labourers. *The Cape Argus* published this photograph on September 22, 1958. See p. 106.

8. Ruth First illustrated her article in *New Age* with this photograph of three of her informants. They had walked all the way to Johannesburg in their sack clothes, given to them, as the Nazis dressed their concentration camp inmates in special clothes, to make escape difficult. See p. 115.

Elizabeth Kanon, mother of the child, said that while walking towards the bridge with her baby on her back a motor car passed them from behind. As they crossed the bridge they saw a motor car approaching from the front, and they got on to the pavement. The car passed them and then reversed back. They kept on walking. The car reversed for a second time, swung towards them, and bumped against them. The driver looked out of the window and said: 'I did get you after all'. Elizabeth said she got up and felt her child's head and found that it was soft. After taking the baby off her back she discovered it was dead. (S 27/1/57)

Fifty-five labourers were whipped, and one died
On the farm Dwarsfontein, 'it was an every-day occurrence for labourers to be struck with whips and sticks on their way to the lands from the compounds where they were locked up for the night. The indunas (foremen) who were in charge of the labourers, hit them to make them run to work'. And one of the labourers, Ncakemi Mkize, was killed by the indunas on February 8. These were some of the facts that emerged in the trial of Max Mann and Willem Johannes Pieters, with five indunas of the farm Dwarsfontein, in the Delmas district, eastern Transvaal.

One of the witnesses, a 15-year-old boy named Johannes Mamela, said that on Saturday the labourers worked until 4 p.m., and were then locked into a room. They stayed locked in that room until the Monday morning. The police evidence was that 'the room had all the appearance of a prison'.

Mamela said that he had been assaulted at work by indunas. He showed the court a scar across his face which, he said, had been caused by the indunas. 'The point of the whip caught me in the eye and I could not see all day', he said.

Mamela said that Pieters nearly killed him with a whip, and

that he used the whip more than the indunas did. Mamela had seen a labourer assaulted by the indunas and by the farmers. 'He was unconscious, and I thought he was dead. As he was lying on his back Mann came and kicked him in the stomach. He lay there for quite a while. Then I saw him get up again. He complained to (one of the indunas) who said he was a liar and started hitting him again. Mokwena and Molife (indunas) also attacked him, but later left him alone.' Mamela said that he saw Mann assault one of the labourers with a pick. The labourer became unconscious, but when he got up he was again assaulted. He complained to Mann, who hit him with a whip. He again got up, started work again, but was assaulted by Pieters and the indunas. He remembered seeing Mann assault an African named Stanley with a pick handle. Stanley was at the time of the hearing in hospital.

In all, fifty-five labourers were whipped.

As a result of complaints the police went out to Dwarsfontein, and one of them, Sergeant Nel, found 106 Africans working on the lands, wearing sacks. Out of the 106, 52 had wounds on their bodies and legs. Pieters told the sergeant that the workers were given sacks to wear so that they would not run away. (S 21, 22/2/51; 17, 18/5/51)

'Wait, let me show you how one hits a kaffir . . .'
And the answer, apparently, is that one hits him with a wire rope, bangs his head on the ground, and kills him.

In his lifetime Andries Sehule worked on the farm Sandspruit, in the Muldersdrif district of the Transvaal. His employer was Stephanus Lodewyk van Zyl. Van Zyl, one Andries Lubbe, and an unnamed white youth, chased Sehule after there had been some trouble. The youth caught him and brought him down. Lubbe hit Sehule on the stomach with a piece of wire rope, while Sehule lay on his back. (Not even

dogs are accustomed to continue a fight if one of the com-
batants lies on its back.) The youth hit Sehule in the face with
his fist and also kicked him.

Van Zyl hit Sehule in the face with the flat of his hand.
Lubbe then said: 'Wait, let me show you how a person hits a
kaffir'. He then lifted Sehule up to his feet and banged his
head on the ground.

The whites then went away. Sehule remained, lying on the
ground. The Africans carried him to his room. He could not
speak. He breathed fast. His eyes were open. There was a
wound on his head. His lip was cut and was bleeding. The
police came in a '*vangwa*' (catch-waggon, meaning a pick-up
truck), and took Sehule away, to die. (B 29/3/62)

These last two cases are of interest in one way: they were
both reported in the nationalist press, for *Die Burger* supports
the government in most things. If proof were needed that decent
whites do not approve the atrocities recorded here, this is it.
What is wanting in both the Afrikaans government-supporting
press, and the anti-government English press, is an understand-
ing that white South Africa as a whole is guilty, because to
deprive Africans as a whole of status and power and dignity
in the country as a whole is to hand individual African workers
over to the uncontrolled power of certain whites. And, such is
the tribal hatred of whites for Africans, and vice versa, that
some among the thousands of farmers in this position of unquestioned power behave like nazi thugs.

White South Africa hands powerless men and women and
children over to the powerful who hate them. White South
Africa as a whole must therefore take a goodly part of the responsibility for what inevitably happens. The only remedy is
that the powerless must be given power, and, in 1964 terms,
this means the vote.

Beating naked girls

If you are a black girl aged 14, and you commit the atrocious crime of climbing through a white farmer's fence in order to pick up dried cowdung for fuel (for that is all the fuel many Africans have on the South African high veld), what punishment is suitable for you? Hendrik Petrus Steenkamp, of the farm Nooitgedacht, Welkom district, thought he knew the answer.

With two African labourers and his dogs in his van he drove up to the children as they were collecting the dung. Steenkamp ordered them to get into the van and lie down so that people could not see them. Then the van stopped in the veld. One of the African labourers ordered the girls to get out of the van. She was ordered to undress and told to lie on her stomach on the van with her legs hanging over the edge.

One of the Africans held her feet. Then Steenkamp took a length of rubber hose out of a box and beat her. He beat her 16 times.

The same happened to another girl.

The magistrate said that Steenkamp should not have taken the law into his own hands, and sentenced him to a fine of £5. (RDM 18/5/62)

Tyrannous caprice

The essential nature of tyranny is that it is capricious. The despot chops the victim's head off because he does not like a wart on the man's nose.

Many – perhaps thousands – of tyrants are today to be found on South African farms. One of them killed a man in 1962 on the farm Springfontein near Merweville, Cape. His name is Jacobus Lodewikus Erasmus. He is aged 37.

On March 6, 1962 Erasmus felt sick. He had also had an argument with his father about the shearing of sheep. He was also apparently dissatisfied with the way in which one of his workers, Floors Alexander, a coloured man, was sorting the wool.

After lunch Alexander was sorting wool at one side of a wool-sack. Erasmus was standing near him, cleaning his fingernails with a knife.

With no warning, and nothing said, and no quarrel, and in a sudden fit of temper, Erasmus stabbed Alexander with the knife and killed him.

But Alexander did not die immediately. He was left lying there for four hours until he died. The judge, Judge Herbstein, commented: 'Erasmus took no steps to call a doctor. When he telephoned the police about the incident he was told to bring the man into town. But he did nothing, and went and lay on his bed. In the meantime the man was bleeding internally, from which he died. The attitude towards him was callous in the extreme.'

Judge Herbstein sentenced Erasmus to six years' imprisonment, of which two were suspended, and ordered him to pay £190 to the widow. (S 18/5/62)

Erasmus was guilty. In many other lands he would have hanged. But the blame is not all his. If he treated Floors Alexander as a thing of little worth the reason lies in the basic constitution of the Union of South Africa which tells all the non-whites that they do not count for anything in the eyes of the state. It tells them this by denying them the vote because their skins are dark. And that constitution was an Act of the British parliament. And that constitution was made because earlier, in the peace treaty of Vereeniging, the British promised the defeated Boers that they could have the vote, but that Britain would not give the Africans the vote. Thus the Africans were delivered, bound hand and foot, to the white settlers of South Africa.

'*The cow's in the meadow, the sheep in the corn*'

An assault by motor car was committed on a herdboy of 14 years of age who worked for Willem Jacobus Smit Enslin, of Nooitgedacht, Middelburg, Transvaal. Some of the cattle he was herding went astray in the croplands. The employer drove over in his car in the direction in which the herdboy was. As he approached the boy he drove slowly. The boy was frightened, and began to run. The employer chased him in his car. Then he swerved deliberately and bumped the boy, inflicting serious injuries to him. The boy spent a month in hospital recovering from the assault.

The judge found Enslin guilty and sentenced him to two months' imprisonment without the option of a fine. (S 27/8/54)

An accident

Johan Willem Christiaan van Staden, aged 30, of Schuinsdrif, Marico, killed a little African girl named Keke, aged six, with a gunshot, and injured a little African child of two behind the right ear with the same shot.

But he did not do it deliberately. It was an accident. Van Staden had actually fired at a grown-up called Isak Molela because Molela, not having had his customary mid-day food, had gone to the house and asked for it. (S 30/8/54)

Brutality learned by immigrants

The nazis were never short of foreigners who quickly learned that atrocious cruelty was part of the system, and sometimes outdid the Germans at their own game.

So it is in Southern Africa. Often the immigrants are crueller than the born white South Africans, just as converts are often more catholic than the Pope.

Be this as it may, Jan Wilhelm Lucius Sybes, a Dutch immigrant farmer of Margate, Natal, proved himself no whit inferior to the best local thugs in 1954. Some of Sybes's cattle had been found damaging corn on a neighbour's farm. Two herdsmen drove the cattle towards the pound, according to law. Sybes intercepted them and tried to stop them from driving the cattle to the pound. There followed an argument. Sybes shot the two men dead. Naturally they were unarmed, being Africans.

Sybes was sentenced to three years in prison. (DD 18/5/54)

How to die when you are chained to a ladder
Marthinus Johannes Celliers, a 21-year-old farmer from Dundee, Natal, burst into tears as he and his father, Marthinus Celliers, were sentenced to 12 years' imprisonment for a 'cruel and prolonged' assault on Alfios Sibisi who died after 18 hours of beatings and ill-treatment. 'The behaviour ... was cruel, unmerciful and the torture stretched over a period of 18 hours. ... Sibisi had been beaten with hosepipes, tied, kicked, and left chained up for a whole night without food. ... He died the next day while still chained to a ladder with a 14-pound tractor chain', said the judge, Judge James, in sentencing them.

What caused such torture? An axe went missing on the Celliers farm, Sheepridge, in the Dundee district, Natal, and Sibisi said that he had taken it.

The younger Celliers then took a knobkerrie (stick with large round knob on one end used as a club) and struck Sibisi with it on the head. He bled. Sibisi cried out and fell to the ground after the younger Celliers struck him a number of times. After that Sibisi did not speak, but he wept.

Sibisi was then taken to a kraal (cattle-enclosure) where the younger Celliers tied his hands with a riem and made him climb into the back of a pick-up van. The two Celliers then drove to the huts of a man named Mtini. They got out, and walked to the huts. The younger Celliers again hit Sibisi. The party did not find the axe at Mtini's, so they all returned to the farm. Sibisi was tied spread-eagled to two poles in a stable. The younger Celliers then went to the house and returned with three pieces of rubber piping and a torch. He handed a piece of piping to his father, and to another white person, Anthony Marcus Meyer, of Pongola, a guest staying with the Celliers family.

'The Europeans then hit Sibisi on the buttocks with the piping until late in the evening. The younger Celliers warned Sibisi that he was not to make a noise. After the beating, the elder Celliers went to the house and returned with a bucket of warm water which he threw over Sibisi's buttocks.'

Sibisi was told to take off his clothes, and the younger Celliers fetched a chain. Sibisi was locked to a ladder and the boy and another umfaan were told to sleep with him in the stable that night. Sibisi groaned during the night.

After breakfast the next day, Sibisi was again taken to look for the missing axe at his kraal, but without success.

On their return to Sheepridge, Sibisi was again tied up in the stable.

The younger Celliers took two railway sleepers and placed them flat on the ground parallel to one another and at right angles to the two poles used the night before, so as to form a rectangle.

The three Europeans then fastened Sibisi to the sleepers by his hands and feet.

The boy and another labourer who were in the stable were then sent to a kraal, and while they were there they heard Sibisi being beaten. He was crying.

When they returned to the stable, the boy said, he saw Sibisi lying on the floor. He had been released from the sleepers and was chained to the ladder again.

Later that day the boy found that Sibisi was dead. He was still chained to the ladder.   (CT 1/3/62, RDM 5/6/62)

One of the witnesses told the court that before he died Sibisi said: 'O dear mother, I am being done for today'. The value of the missing axe was £1.5.9.

Torture by fire and electricity
Kleinbooi Mpeku, an employee of Francois Alwyn du Preez, a white farmer of the Pietersburg district, Transvaal, was accused by his employer of stealing £624 from a store on his farm. Du Preez took Mpeku to the police, but the police could prove nothing. On the day the police released him Du Preez called for him in his motor car and took him to his farm. Accompanied by an African employee Du Preez took Mpeku out into the veld. They asked him to show them where the stolen money was hidden. He failed to do this. So they began to torture him to get him to talk.

First they bound his hands, and drove thorns into his fingernails. Then electric leads from a car were fastened to his face and his penis, and the engine of the car was started. Then his feet were roasted over a specially prepared fire.

The fire charred the bones of one foot. Later three toes and part of the foot had to be amputated by a doctor.

The judge said that it was accepted that there had been serious provocation, since Du Preez owed the stolen money to wholesalers and Mpeku had a previous conviction for theft from Du Preez's store. People could nevertheless not take the law into their own hands. He therefore sentenced Du Preez to 18 months' imprisonment, of which nine months were suspended, and four strokes. (PN 30/4/57)

CHAPTER TWELVE

Legal Background to Farm Labour

African farm workers can be divided into two principal categories: workers placed on farms by the law-enforcement system, and those whose presence on farms is not due to the law-enforcement system.

The first category might be called 'unfree', and the second 'free'. But the word 'free' is quite inappropriate to describe African farm labourers anywhere in South Africa.

The law enforcement system places workers on farms in several ways. Firstly, there is the farm jail system. In this system, farmers build jails privately; the prison department staffs and fills the jails; and the prisoners are hired out to farmers at 1s 9d a day. Secondly, the farmers may recruit convicts to be their own labourers. Thirdly, there was an infamous scheme under which the authorities illegally pressed persons who had been arrested into taking contracts with farmers in lieu of prosecution. This, for the sake of brevity, we shall call the 'Fordsburg' scheme.

Those are the three ways in which the law enforcement system places African workers on white men's farms. More information will be given below.

Then there are two main ways in which African workers work on white farms without the intervention of the law-enforcement system.

Firstly, there is the system of wage-labourers. These are either born on the farm, or move on to it from elsewhere, or are contracted by recruiting agents and are brought to the farm. Secondly, there is the system of unpaid labour, the squatting system. Under this system the labourers and their children are compelled to labour for up to six months for the white farmer for no reward except the right to stay on the farm and perhaps to cultivate some small plots on it. Most of these labourers were born on their farms. Indeed many of these squatting families have been on that land for generations longer than the white owners.

It will be convenient now to deal with each of these categories in order.

The Farm Jail System

This system, and the others to be mentioned, is fully and fairly described in a memorandum produced by the South African Institute of Race Relations (reference: RR 153/59). It was also described in 1960 in an authoritative article in *Contact* by Myrna Blumberg. In this article she described how farmers had been encouraged by the government to form unique organizations known as Farmers' Prison Co-operative Societies. And she described how these societies built unique establishments, privately-owned prisons. I quote from this article:

> There are now over ten farm jails in the Cape alone; 13 in the Transvaal and two in the Orange Free State.
>
> A government official in Paarl recently told a farmer I know, 'The South African wine industry would collapse without convict labour'.
>
> How does one go about getting a farm jail?
>
> Farmers in need of labour get together to form a Prison Co-operative and jointly raise the money – anything from £20,000 to £75,000 – to build a jail in a spot convenient to them all. The Prisons Department then fills it up with African men on short-term sentences – men arrested for trivial technicalities like not having their passes on them, being in arrears with taxes, being in a town without written permission from a white official. White man-made offences that make criminals of black men only.
>
> Every morning before 7 a.m. the farmers come to load

the men into their vans. They deposit with the prison authorities 1s 9d a day a convict if they supply their own armed guard; 2s a day a convict if they require a guard from the Prisons Department.

The convicts work until 5 p.m. usually, on the normal African prison diet of mealie-meal porridge, vegetables and meat three times a week.

The prison authorities supply the food as well as the staff in the jail itself. The farmers maintain the jail, paying for electricity and so on.

Obviously, it must be worth it. A report in the *Cape Times* of May 27, 1959, coming from its George correspondent, said, 'Farmers, for the first time, can use to advantage the benefits of the new and imposing jail here . . .

'The complement of convicts has been increased to 170, and this ready supply of labour will counteract the scarcity of farm labour which has been experienced in the past years . . .

'The convict labour is far cheaper, as farmers pay between 1s 7d and 1s 9d a day – as against 6s and 8s a day.'

On February 25, 1958, Mr V. R. Verster, Director of Prisons, was reported as saying, 'The Department of Prisons has become the focal point to farmers from the Limpopo to Cape Town.'

The chain of jails, spreading like an infectious rash over the countryside, owe their real inspiration to C. R. Swart, who has just been appointed governor-general.

In August, 1952, Swart said that farm jails were his 'own particular baby'.

He nurtured and encouraged them, and in 1957 declared that they were not only helping farmers, but providing an income for the state and rehabilitation for the prisoners.

(C 23/1/60)

One of the Cape farm jails was built by one single farmer, Cecil Morgan, a wealthy poultry farmer at Soete Inval, Stikland, near Cape Town. His family is related to that of Charles Robberts Swart, the president, and he is on good terms with cabinet ministers. Instructions have been given verbally to the Cape Town prisons department that everything must be done, and no expense spared, to see that the Morgan jail is always full of convicts, and that it is efficiently run.

Contact obtained photographs of the Morgan house and of two convicts working mending the farm fence. But the jail itself is built away from the road, and a policeman on a bicycle patrolled the nearby public road all the time, making it impossible for the photographer to get any other photographs.

Under the prisons laws it is illegal for any prison or prison staff or prisoner to be photographed without the permission of the department.

And when thieves approach the farm at night, the police defences are good. They shot a man dead on this farm at 11 p.m. on March 23, 1962. Five fowls were found with him. In South Africa this justified his being killed. (A 24/3/62)

Schemes by which farmers recruit prison labour
Secondly, as we saw above, farmers may recruit convicts in jail to be their labourers. They do so in three ways.

'Firstly the farmer may interview Africans who are serving sentences in lieu of payment of fines, and, should he find a man who is willing to enter his employment at current rates of pay, may apply for suspension of the sentence on condition that the prisoner remains in his employment for the unexpired portion of his sentence or until he has earned enough to pay the fine. Secondly, a prisoner serving a sentence of three months or less may, if he is willing, be released on probation and enter into an approved contract to work for a farmer for the unexpired portion of his sentence at a wage of not less than 9d a day. And thirdly, a first offender

109

serving a sentence of from one to two years may be invited after completion of half of his sentence to work for a farmer for the remaining portion at locally-prevailing wage rates.'

(C 28/11/59)

Under these schemes the convicts are at the mercy of the farmers. The Race Relations memorandum quotes several assault cases, of which two are recorded here:

(a) A farmer, G. S. Lourens, of the Standerton District, was during May 1959, found guilty of assaulting convict labourers, and was sentenced to a fine of £50 (or four months' imprisonment), a further two months' imprisonment being conditionally suspended for three years. (*Rand Daily Mail* report, May 28, 1959.)

(b) A *habeas corpus* application was made by Rachel Madeira, during June 1959, for the return of her husband Gabriel from the farm of C. F. Grobler in the Trichardt District. She stated that Gabriel had been retained on the farm beyond the date when his sentence expired to make up for a period when he was ill. Gabriel was in hospital at the time when his application came before the Supreme Court, Pretoria: it was alleged that he was assaulted on the farm after he had visited a police station to request that he be discharged. (*Star* reports, June 24 and 25, 1959.)

(C 28/11/59)

The 'Fordsburg' Scheme

Thirdly, as we saw above, there was an infamous scheme under which the authorities illegally pressed persons arrested, but not charged or convicted, into contracting themselves for three and six months on the farms. The old native commissioner's office, Fordsburg, was the place where most of these contracts were signed, and so the scheme may conveniently be called the 'Fordsburg' scheme.

Individuals and newspapers attacked the scheme, and so

many unpleasant facts became known about it that it was withdrawn in 1959. The authorities have not dared reintroduce it. Readers must not therefore suppose that the abuses under this scheme are happening now: they must read the details of this scheme to know that, if they can get away with it, the apartheid authorities do not shrink from oppression and even illegality to help their farmer friends. But readers must also read the details of this scheme with hope: that it is not impossible, even in these dark days, for public opinion, white as well as non-white, to be mobilized effectively to stop abuses, and that even today the government is capable of reacting to public opinion to halt the excesses of apartheid.

Of all the opponents of the scheme none stands out with greater lustre than does Joel Carlson, a young Johannesburg attorney. Many years before this scheme was withdrawn Carlson had been disturbed by this practice. 'It was like a slave market', he told one newspaper, 'with farmers begging for batches of arrested men to take away as labourers'.

What, in essence, was the 'Fordsburg' scheme? In 1954 the secretary for native affairs, with the concurrence of the secretary for justice and the commissioner of police, issued a circular ordering magistrates and police officers to '*induce* (my emphasis) unemployed natives roaming about the streets in various urban areas to accept employment outside such urban areas'. According to the circular the scheme would save money on the daily arrests and prosecutions of Africans for 'contraventions of a purely technical nature'.

How did it work? Squads of police, not in uniform, but armed, would round up Africans on the streets, and ask for their passes. When people challenged these squads (known as the 'ghost squads') for their credentials they would not produce credentials, but would tap their pistols as credentials, a typical and revealing act. Anyone without a pass would be arrested,

III

put in a pick-up van and taken to cells, and threatened with prosecution. Under the threat of prosecution, the police and magistrates would offer them work. Often the work was described as 'work in a jam factory' or other forms of industrial work. But in fact the only work ever actually given was work on the farms. The men were told that if they signed these contracts, for three and six months, they would not be prosecuted. Many thousands signed, or merely joined queues of men who understood nothing except that they were being driven on to lorries to avoid prison.

The scheme was illegal. A man may not be arrested unless the police believe that he has committed an offence. Their clear duty is then to place him before a court for his guilt to be determined. To interfere with this clear process for any consideration is to commit the crime of compounding an offence.

The scheme was tyrannical and corrupt, for it degraded the police from being law enforcement officers into being kidnappers and blackbirders.

The scheme led to the disappearance of people. Often their relatives had no means of tracing them, and they disappeared for months. It led to brutalities, naturally.

'A serious case of ill-treatment of petty offenders was reported in the Press during August and September, 1958. Thirty-two Africans had been sent from the labour bureau to the farm of C. L. S. Botha in the Heidelberg area, and, following alleged thrashings, they decided to leave and report back to the authorities. As they walked along the road a van overtook them, warning shots were fired, and they were rounded up and taken back to the farm, where they were cruelly beaten. Botha was later found guilty of assault with intent to do grievous bodily harm, and was sentenced to 4½ years' imprisonment and seven strokes with a cane.

Two of his white and seven of his African staff received lesser sentences for participating in the assaults.

(C 28/11/59)

The scheme flared into the headlines when Carlson applied for the return of a man named Nelson Langa by bringing an action of *habeas corpus* to the supreme court. These are the facts in this case:

In June 1957 Langa, a cleaner working for the Johannesburg municipality at a wage of £2.8.9 a week, plus board, was walking home from work. At about 3 p.m. some members of the police 'dressed in private clothes' came to him and said 'pass'. (This meant that they were asking him to produce his 'pass' or reference book.) He told them that he had no pass on his person because cleaners did not carry their passes on them when they were at work. He said to them 'Here is my badge with my number on it. And I am carrying my broom that I use in my work'. But they said: 'We have nothing to do with that. Get off to the lorry'.

The people who questioned him were in groups. There were both whites and Africans in the groups. None were in uniform. The lorry, with a number of other Africans, some of whom were picked up on the way, was driven to Regent's Park, where they spent the night.

The next morning they were taken to the old pass office in Johannesburg. There the name of each was taken, and they were told that they were going to be given work. Langa said: 'I don't want to be given work. I am already working'. A clerk said: 'We have nothing to do with that. You will be given work'. The following day they were put on a truck and taken to Bethal.

(The Bethal area is notorious for the most unpleasant conditions in South Africa for farm labourers.)

Bethal is 100 miles away from Johannesburg, where Langa worked.

By chance Nelson Langa's brother, Innocent Langa, learned that he had been taken to the farm of a farmer named Max Hirschowitz, whose address is Scheepers Street, Bethal. He was being paid £3 for 30 working days' work (i.e. more than a month).

Joel Carlson had for years been disturbed by this practice. When Innocent Langa came to him and told him about his brother's disappearance he agreed to take the matter up.

Represented by Carlson, Innocent Langa went to the Supreme Court and asked for a *habeas corpus* order calling on Max Hirschowitz to produce the body of Nelson Langa.

Here are some of the things that appeared in this application:

That Nelson Langa had not fetched his clothes, and had failed to collect his pay.

That he had not given notice to the municipality and could thus be prosecuted for desertion.

That this case was one of many in which Africans were coerced into entering into so-called 'voluntary' contracts for farm labour, agreements which were really induced by threats of prosecution.

That such contracts were generally for three to six months, whereas the law only provided for a £1 fine or 14 days in prison for failing to produce a pass.

The judge, Judge Rumpff, ordered that Nelson Langa be immediately released.

An appeal was noted. Incredibly, although Max Hirschowtiz, the respondent, was a private person, the appeal was taken by the government's legal representative, the state attorney.

On October 21, 1958, the day before the appeal was due to

be heard, the state attorney, acting on behalf of Max Hirsch-owitz, and of the native commissioner of Johannesburg, aban-doned his appeal. Government was ordered to pay costs.

One of the first newspapers to expose this scandal of the 'Fordsburg' scheme was the communist weekly, now suppres-sed, *New Age*. In the issue of September 1, 1955, there appeared an account, by Ruth First, a staffer, of an investigation of this scheme.

At the time of writing (December 1963) Ruth First has just been released from prison after a prolonged period of detention under the 90-day clause for interrogation. Separated from her husband and her children, no one doubts that she resisted her inquisitors dauntlessly.

In 1955, her story was published under the headline: 'Lab-our Bureau tricks Africans into going to Farms'. I give it in full:

> Those who are so quick to deny that there is forced labour in South Africa should have been in Alexandra Township in the late afternoon of Wednesday, August 24. Nine Afri-cans arrived in the township, bruised, ill, footsore and ex-hausted. They had walked all the way from Devon, halfway between Bethal and Johannesburg.
>
> All were dressed in sacks, like the three shown in the picture: holes torn in the grain bags for head and arm openings, the 'uniform' of thousands of wretched farm workers on the rich mealie and potato farms of the eastern Transvaal.
>
> This is what they told me:
>
> All nine were arrested in Alexandra Township during June of this year, some on June 18, others a little later in the month. They were arrested under the pass laws, some picked up in police street raids, others in yard searches.
>
> They were taken to the Wynberg police station, and from there to the Native Labour Bureau. There, they said, they

were offered work in a Germiston iron and steel factory.

One of the nine, a tailor by trade, told me he never believed that they were being sent to a factory: he knew it would be on a farm. The others believed they were going to work in a factory. The nine say that they signed no contracts, and put their fingerprints to no document.

The day after their arrest and the offer of work to them, a lorry arrived outside the office of the Wynberg Native Commissioner. They climbed aboard and the lorry started off. To the astonishment of all but the tailor the lorry passed right through Germiston, and stopped at last on a farm in the Devon district. 'Here you work,' the nine were told.

They were on the farm of Mr X (the name is in our possession), one of the biggest farmers in the district.

The nine worked for one month on the farm: the work was from 'Sunday to Sunday,' they said. On the same farm were a number of other African men, also from Alexandra Township. At the end of one month some went to the farmer to ask to be sent back home, as they believed they had worked their 'term'.

The farmer told them they could not leave, and they had to work a second month, as notice.

At the end of the second month nine men went again to the farmer. By this time some had worked for two months, some for two months and 15 days, and some for two months and 23 days. The farmer again refused to let the nine go, or to pay them, or return their pass reference books.

The nine left the farm and reported to the Devon police station.

They were given no help but told they should report to the centre from where they had been sent to Devon. So the nine took to the road and walked back to Alexandra Township. When they arrived they were wearing the sacking used as clothing on the farm.

Several immediately reported to the Township clinic for

medical treatment for the bruises on their bodies, evidence of the assaults on them on the farm.

Two of the men are only 18 years old, one is 19. One of the 18-year-olds was born in Alexandra Township, went to school there for a few years and after leaving school in 1953 was one of the youngsters of the township desperate to work, who found his way to employment blocked at every turn by the influx control and pass regulations which doom so many young men in Alexandra Township to a life of despair, hunted by the police and haunted by the prospect of having to work on the farms for a pittance.

Another of the nine was a man 47 years old, a married man and father of one child, a registered tenant in Orlando, he told *New Age*, and a tailor who has worked in Johannesburg since 1937.

One of the 18-year-olds has a large bruise on one side of his face, and a scab, now healing, on his right arm. Both injuries were caused by a sjambok, he said.

All nine reported to the offices of the Labour Bureau and the Native Commissioner for their pass books and the money owed them for their work on the farm.

Later the following afternoon, after *New Age* had interviewed and photographed them and they had given statements to a lawyer alleging they had been assaulted and misled about the work to be offered them, their former farmer employer drove personally into the Township from his Devon farm and paid the nine out.

The sight of *New Age* photographing three Africans in sacking, on the pavement opposite the Native Commissioner's offices, brought the Township Labour Bureau officer over.

Why were we dressing these people in sacks, he asked us? We made an explanation, but he insisted that he didn't consider it 'cricket' to take pictures of men wearing sacks!

Later, before the Native Commissioner, the Labour Officer explained that his Bureau handled at least 100 Africans from the township a day, offering them work. Only the day before 16 had been sent to work on farms, but three had already returned to the Township. The trouble was, he said, that these men did not really want to work!

As for Mr X of Devon, he was a very big farmer in that district, and got a great deal of his labour from the Bureau in the Township, said the Labour officer.

The people in the Township well know that more farmers than one get regular supplies of labour from the Township's bureau. The hunt for Africans under the pass laws goes on apace, and twice a week lorries from the platteland draw up outside the offices of the Labour Bureau and groups of Africans are ushered aboard.

Then they disappear into the countryside, some to return after only a short period when they desert, others after some months.

In its issue of June 23, *New Age* told the story of Mr M—— who was shipped off to work on a farm in the Springs district although he had in his possession a legal permit to seek work. He told of how during his detention by the police he was presented with an ultimatum to accept work on a farm or be sent to the Leeuwkop Farm Colony.

To how many people in the Township is this same ultimatum put?

So much for the permitted recruitment of farm labour by the law-enforcement system. But when power on a great scale is put into the hands of minor functionaries, abuses crowd in. And there is a good deal of illegal pressing of Africans into unpaid labour on farms.

The most notorious case is the case of Le Roux, an official in the Paarl, Cape, locations system. He used to intimidate Africans into working on his farm for nothing for two weeks. Or else he would illegally give benefits administratively to others who agreed to work for him for nothing. For instance he would 'fix' their passes for them, if they agreed to work for him for nothing.

Most Africans, the overwhelming majority, however, are not placed in their farm work by the law enforcement system. As seen above, they work for cash, or for the right to occupy their homes.

Wage labourers

When I lived at Riverside, Ladybrand district, near Maseru, Basutoland, in about 1957, the grown-up labourers in that area of the Orange Free State used to get, in cash, from £1.5 to £1.15 a month. If a man were a tractor-driver, he might get a pound more each month. In addition, depending on the goodwill of the employer, a man would be given food. A normal ration was 90 lb of mealie meal (maize meal) monthly plus some skimmed milk daily. Some farmers gave meat (boys' meat as it is ambiguously termed in the Free State butcheries, meaning the worst, oldest, boniest, and thinnest cuts).

In addition, the labourer was responsible for building his own house. He might never, under the Land Act of 1913, own outright one square foot of the farm, but he was expected to build and maintain his own house. If he left, he might take the roof, if the roof were portable, and the windows and doors.

And his duties were to work every weekday of the year from '*sonop*' (sunrise) to '*sononder*', except Christmas, New Year and Good Friday. Normally public holidays were not allowed to farm workers, nor, naturally, were farm workers entitled to paid holidays. Nor, under the masters and servants laws that regulated their lives, were they entitled to anything. *Per contra*, they could be prosecuted if they left their employment.

Why, if conditions were so bad, it might be asked, did they not leave and go to the towns? There are two main reasons. Firstly, under the pass laws, it is normally illegal for an African to exist anywhere without the permission of the white boss of the locality. And the only places an African farm worker can move to are other farms or locations (townships for Africans). But no African may go on to another farm without the permission of the farmer, nor into a location without the permission of the location superintendent. This permission would not be given unless the African had a satisfactory letter from his late employer. Thus, by withholding such a 'pass' the employer could prevent a man from leaving the farm.

But the second reason is the main one: the government is a farmers' government. The farmers need what they call 'abundant native labour'. It irritated them when in the earlier years Africans were able to go to the cities and the mines. So government stepped in with its 'influx control' and made it illegal for an African to move to any town in South Africa without permission from the authorities of that town. And, now Verwoerd is prime minister, government policy has been not only to refuse such permission to farm workers, but, in so far as has been in the government's power, they have used their vast powers to return African farm workers from the cities to the farms.

And so, since the nationalist victory of 1948, the Free State farms have bulged with unwanted, unemployed and under-employed people. On an Orange Free State farm of about nine hundred acres two white families lived in 1960, with between a hundred and a hundred and twenty Africans. As the young men grew up they would beg the white farmer for work, but he was often unable to give them work. They begged for passes to go to the cities and find work there, but they could not do this, as the local magistrate, instructed by the Verwoerd government, refused permission. And so they sat around the farm, under-fed and hopeless.

And that is how most Africans live who are born on a Free State farm.

'Squatters'

But the other system is far worse, the squatting system. How did people become squatters in the beginning? The normal way was when, perhaps eighty or a hundred years ago, one of the governments proclaimed certain tracts of land which had been lived on by Africans for centuries, to be 'Crown Land'. Then, in some distant deeds registry, the government would give, or sell, this land to a white aspirant farmer. This man would go to the portion of land, and tell the Africans that henceforth they must work for him. One man described such a moment graphically: 'One day my father woke up in his own house, on land that had been ours for many generations. Outside his house stood a white man. The white man said: "You are living on my land. In future you must work for me".'

Some of these squatters are compelled by law to work for six months, they and their wives and children, for the farmer for nothing except the right to occupy their homes, and perhaps their plots too. Even if they go to a town to take up other work they are compellable to return each year to the farm to work for the farmer, for nothing.

Especially in Natal, where this system is widespread, white farmers buy farms because of the quantities of labourers tied to them in this way. They then use them on this, and perhaps on other farms, getting their labour on these other farms too, free and without paying one penny in wages.

An interesting letter describing this system, and the secrecy with which it is surrounded, appeared in *The Observer* recently:

> Sir,—Let me tell you of my own experience in South Africa, as a British subject who refuses to interfere in South African politics, but who does like to know the truth.
>
> I married a South African girl some years ago, and in 1961, while we were visiting her parents who live in a small country town near Johannesburg, I found that one of the

African servants had to spend six months of every year working free for a local farmer. A few questions, and I had the reason.

The lad's parents had 'squatted' on the farm before he was born, and under South African law the farmer 'owned' the lad for six months every year for life. Thus, after six months working for my in-laws, the young African would have to work for six months free for the farmer.

I investigated this matter with the local office of the Bantu Administration Department, who merely looked surprised and said it was legal. So I wrote to a Johannesburg newspaper about it. The reaction was immediate. A senior official of the Bantu Administration Department told me I was talking rubbish, and inferred that I should keep my nose out of South Africa's affairs. Three days later, I had an anonymous phone call in which I was told, quite courteously, to stop writing to the Press about such things – or else.

This is but one of many examples of the extraordinary discrepancy between South African facts and South African official statements.

BRITISHER

Cape Town   (O 17/11/63)

Some farmers built up huge holdings of squatters, thus earning the envy of many other farmers, perhaps farmers with more influence in this farmers' government. And so the government, predictably, has stepped in.

Labour Tenants' Control Boards were set up in about 1958 to determine the number of families of labour tenants that may be employed on each farm within their area of jurisdiction. (A labour tenant is a squatter.)

According to Verwoerd, while he was minister of native affairs, speaking in the Assembly on July 11, 1958, those labour tenants who are considered to be surplus to requirements are being assisted by labour bureaux to re-settle on other farms where workers are needed. Squatters requiring employment are being assisted to obtain work as full-time farm workers.

What, behind these smooth and untruthful euphemisms, does this mean to the squatters and farm labourers generally? It means, of course, that their only defence is taken away from them. In the past, African labourers have usually contrived to keep away from the worst farmers, from the farmers who assault or kill labourers, or who pay even less than the normal wages. These farmers have for years pestered the government to compel Africans to work for them. The setting-up of the Labour Tenants' Control Bureaux was to satisfy this, the most unsatisfactory and dissatisfied element among the white farmers. So now, if labour stays away from the farm of Mr. X, perhaps because he is cruel or mean, a bureau will 'assist' labourers to 'obtain work' on his farm, having removed them first from land that might well have been in their families for centuries.

The Race Relations memorandum commented that 'it is clear that the implementation of chapter IV of (the Native Trust and Land Amendment) Act is inevitably causing the uprooting and serious dislocation of the lives of many African families. Particular difficulties are likely to be experienced by aged and infirm persons, and by families who own stock'. The reason for this last remark is that, of course, the farmer to whom the labourer is directed may well refuse to take his cattle with him. And in such cases the man is legally compelled to get rid of his cattle, the wealth of the ancestors, the bride-price for his sons, perhaps the bride-price recently brought to the family by the marriage of a daughter.

These are, briefly sketched, the legal disabilities under which African farm labourers suffer. It is in a climate of opinion created by such laws that these fearful tortures and assaults and murders are committed. And the white man's government passes laws like that because the white man has the vote and the black man does not have the vote, because the black man's tribe is completely in the power of the other tribe, the white tribe, that does not like him.

One aspect of violence on the farms remains to be dealt with: the treatment of children. An African farm child is seen by the authorities and the white farmers under two aspects: a future docile labourer, and, in the present, a child-labourer. Education for the farm child must therefore not only fit him for his future subservient place in society, but must also be so arranged that during school hours he can work for the owner of the land on which the farm school is built.

CHAPTER THIRTEEN

Child Labour, 1964 Style

In his pamphlet explaining that in future the African children would not get education as it is universally understood, the opening of channels to give minds a chance to realize their greatest potentialities, but would instead get 'Bantu Education', Verwoerd, then minister of native affairs, used the following words:

'When I have control of Native education I will reform it so that Natives will be taught from childhood to realize that equality with Europeans is not for them. . . . People who believe in equality are not desirable teachers for Natives. When my department controls Native education it will know for what class of higher education a Native is fitted and whether he will have a chance in life to use his knowledge.' (Bantu Education debate in parliament, quoted in *South Africa: Let the Facts Speak*, by Bishop Ambrose Reeves, Christian Action, 1962.)

As shown in *Education for Barbarism* (by I. Tabata) the curriculum was altered with the advent of 'Bantu' education. More time was given for religious instruction and labour. Most time was given to manual training. In the event 'manual training' on farm schools has turned out to mean work, for nothing, on the lands of the farmers.

The minister of Bantu education made no bones about this. In a speech to the Senate at the end of the 1959 parliamentary session he used these words: 'As regards farm schools, we have made it compulsory that where the farmer wants these facilities, part of the school instruction of those (African) children on the farm of the European farmer must be training in the normal activities on the farm, in order to encourage a feeling of industriousness on the part of those children. . . . In order to do this we create the opportunity so that if there is any farmer who has a farm school on his farm and who wishes to make use of the school children under the supervision of the teacher to assist with certain farm activities, this can be arranged in a proper manner to fit in with the curriculum . . . for that farm school'. (C 31/10/59)

What these somewhat euphemistic phrases mean in practice is shown by this report which appeared in a reputable weekly:

Small hands digging in the icy ground, when they should have been pushing pencils over notebooks in school. . . . That is a common and sad sight in the Free State. This is what a reporter of *The World* learned when he went to Kroonstad on Monday to investigate reports.

Many Free State children no longer go to school at all. Others go to school but their class hours are limited by farm work.

At Kroonstad children are helping reap groundnuts, maize and other crops; herding cattle and sheep and girls do domestic work in farmers' houses.

Parents cannot prevent their children from doing farm work for fear of being victimized.

They can lose their farm jobs and accommodation if they oppose the farmers.

The work involved is long and tedious; the children are given no protective clothing, and they have to work in their own clothes.

On one farm about 10 miles east of Kroonstad, a farmer takes children out of school at any time he wishes.

He pays no regard even to school examinations.

A teacher who served in this school, which he left because of disagreement with the farmer, disclosed to a reporter of *The World* some of the practices carried out by a farmer.

'On one occasion,' he said, 'I was about to start with school examinations when a farmer called. He told me he wanted the boys in my class for work on the lands.

'I told him this would not be possible as the children

126

were writing important examinations. The man went into a rage; he told me he was "boss" and I must listen to him.

'All my efforts to explain the importance of the examination were hopeless. The farmer had his way and the children worked on the lands, for no pay, for a number of days,' he said.

As a result, examinations had to be held all day on Sunday to make up for lost time.

The teacher went on: 'On the farms, the farmers are vested with wide powers over schools, children and teachers. At least that is what farmers themselves tell us.

'A farmer on whose property an African school is built generally becomes manager of the school.

'He may do as he likes with children. He can order them any time he so desires to work on the lands with the teacher as "boss-boy".'

'If he wants the children, no matter what time during school hours, he must have them,' he added.

Teachers who challenge this authority may find themselves without jobs.

On one particular farm near Kroonstad, three teachers have been dismissed because of this.

Once there was a near-fight between a farmer and a teacher. As a result, the teacher was dismissed and the school closed down and was transferred to another farm.

'I want them now before they are exhausted. If you give them to me after school, I will first have to feed them,' said a farmer on one occasion.

Children get no pay, nor are they fed.   (W 16/6/56)

Thus, from childhood itself, that age which should be free of harsh cares and responsibilities, the Africans are subjected to the harsh system, are made aware of their own and their parents' powerlessness, and are relentlessly subjected to the vile system of economic and psychological oppression on which modern South Africa is built.

CHAPTER FOURTEEN

Violence by Individuals

Violence by the police, and violence by farmers have been recorded. There is a third form of violence: violence by ordinary white people against non-whites. Although much of this violence is senseless nearly always the tribal factor enters into it. That is to say: nearly always when violence is used by a white person against a non-white person the element of racial and tribal hatred is present. A white person, seeing an unknown white and an unknown non-white fighting in the street will as often as not join the fight, on the side of the unknown white. And his blows against the non-white will seem to him to be blows struck in defence of the white tribe, and in rightful attack against the hostile, non-white tribe.

That is not to say that the reverse is not also true; the element of tribal hatred is also more often than not present when a non-white strikes a white. But the apartheid policy is responsible for both, for it tries to hold the two tribes separate, and will not let human groups grow closer together, even when they want to.

Also, the violence inflicted on a white by a non-white is not violence which is inflicted in the name of apartheid. As such it forms no part of this book.

Perhaps the best recent example of senseless and reckless violence was the case in which Jasper Johannes Marais, aged 20, was given 18 months' imprisonment for having killed an old coloured man of 84 years of age, Daniel ('Dial') Williams.

Marais was a learner-butcher. The judge said that the old man could not defend himself at all. The story is well told in *Drum* (May, 1963).

Old 'Dial' Williams sat down at the roadside on his way to his tiny wood-and-tin shack. It was the evening of Saturday, October 13 last year, and he'd been to a beer drink.

Within 24 hours he would be dead – but thoughts of death were probably far from his mind.

Behind him was a hedge, and behind the hedge was a house – the house of the man who was to become his killer.

There are two versions of what happened when Marais first saw Mr Williams.

One version is the killer's, sworn to voluntarily before a magistrate after Marais' arrest. (Marais at first denied all knowledge of an assault on Mr Williams, and swore a statement to that effect before Detective-Constable J. E. Trollip, the investigating officer).

When he finally confessed before Mr P. J. Fourie, assistant magistrate at Springs, he said he had been under the influence of liquor on the night of the assault.

He said that he had gone to his home to fetch a tyre and tube for a neighbour's car and had seen a 'Bantu' sitting in front of the hedge.

'I asked him what he was doing, but he didn't answer. So I went into the house and fetched my father's sjambok . . .

'I hit the "Bantu" with the sjambok, then I put it away.'

Then, said Marais, he left. When he returned to the house his victim had gone. Later he heard that the police had taken the old man away.

The other version is given by 70-year-old Mr Swartbooi Mabena, who worked for Marais.

He said he was already in bed that night when Marais called him and told him people were creating a disturbance nearby.

Mr Mabena dressed and accompanied Marais, and later saw Mr Williams sitting on the ground.

Marais took the sjambok and, despite Mr Mabena's pleadings, struck him many times.

'All the time, the coloured man remained sitting on the

ground. While Marais was lashing him and hitting him with his fist, the old man said: "Bhabha, Bhabha", which means "Father, Father". He pleaded with Marais.

'Marais said: "You must say, "please baas".'

Mr Mabena said he had told Marais: 'Master, don't hit him so much. You'll kill him.'

At the trial, the judge asked for evidence from the District Surgeon of Springs, Dr D. C. Bowden, about Mr Williams' injuries after the police had taken the old man to the West Springs Hospital.

Dr Bowden said he found severe contusions of the upper lip, which was bleeding. There was gross swelling of the left eye, neither pupil reacted to light, and there was evidence that Mr Williams had consumed liquor. Also, there was a 'tramline' bruise on his shoulder. Mr Williams was admitted for observation.

Questioned by the judge, Dr Bowden said the lip injuries were likely t o have been caused by a fist or a booted foot. The eye injury could have been caused by a fist or a blunt object.

Then the doctor handed in the post-mortem report on Mr Williams' body. Cause of death was listed as subdural haemorrhage and intra-cerebral haemorrhage and contusion.

'I feel it was the result of multiple blows,' the doctor testified.

The judge: Inflicted how? – They could have been inflicted with a fist, a booted foot and even with some type of object like a stick. There were even haemorrhages under the membrane over the eyes.

The judge: Caused by? – That could have been blows to the eyes, My Lord. The bruise over the shoulder is consistent with a blow from a semi-pliable object, maybe a sjambok or a stick.

The judge: Would you say this was a very severe assault? – Yes, My Lord.

The judge: How long could all this (the assault) have lasted? – That is difficult to say, but in view of the age of this man (Mr Williams) and the injuries found, he must have been subjected to a severe assault. His age would have made it even more severe.

Dr Bowden said that the brain injuries suffered by Mr Williams could have been caused by blows jarring the skull.

Mr Justice Bresler asked Marais if he wanted to question the doctor or challenge his evidence. Marais declined. Then this followed . . .

The judge (to Marais): What would you like to say? – I see my sister is here. I'd like her to talk.

The judge: No, she can't talk. You must. What do you want to say? – She can say it better than me.

The judge: What? – It's only myself, my father and my brother who are at home.

The judge: I want to know about the assault. Do you want to say anything? – No, I don't want to say anything.

The judge: Do you accept the doctor's evidence? – Yes.

Marais pleaded with the judge for leniency, saying that his father was gravely ill in hospital.

Mr Justice Bresler told him: 'I can't think now about your father. That is unfortunate, but you must think of your family before you do things like this. Now you want to go free because your father is sick.'

Marais: But I'm the only supporter in the house.

The judge: That may well be so, but the other man is dead. How do you know that he, too, wasn't the only supporter of other people? Did you hear what the doctor said? Did you understand how the man died?

Marais: Yes, sir.

The judge: Do you know why he's dead?

Marais: Yes, sir.

The judge: The whole of one side of his face was virtually beaten to a pulp. Did you hear the evidence that the State prosecutor read out?

Marais: Yes, sir.

The judge: You see, it was a brutal assault. It is the sort of behaviour that disturbs relationships between the people of our society. You should be an example. What do you do? What do you say?

Marais: I don't want to say anything, sir.

Mr Justice Bresler then pronounced sentence. He said: 'Marais, you have heard the evidence. It was a brutal assault. The dead man was 81 years old (Mr Williams' age as given in court) and couldn't defend himself in the least. There are all sorts of culpable homicide, for some of which sentences are suspended, for some of which eight years' jail and six strokes are imposed, for some of which lesser sentences. But the least sentence I can impose on you is 18 months' jail.'

Jasper Johannes Marais was originally arrested and charged with the murder of Mr Williams. He was committed for trial on the murder charge by Mr A. W. J. Hellferscee, additional magistrate at Springs, at a preparatory examination that ended on November 27 last year. But the charge was subsequently reduced to one of culpable homicide.

There are many, many more cases of this 'private violence', of the injuring and killing for the maintenance of white supremacy. Perhaps one more will be enough. I feel that to place it at the end of this horrible catalogue is in a way appropriate, for it is the first record I decided to keep with the aim, one day, of writing this book.

In 1948 the inhabitants of the small Basutoland village of Teyateyaneng, near the Orange Free State border, were shocked to hear how a young Sotho man, David Masupha, had been recklessly injured by unknown white men. At that time, I was working in the colonial government (under the British colonial office) in Basutoland. Masupha was brought to me and told me his story.

At about 9 o'clock of April 26 he had been walking along the tarred road near the Catholic church in Ficksburg, a small Free State town. A car came along with three white men and a white woman in it. The men were aged about 20 to 24 years.

(It afterwards appeared that the men's names were: Marthinus Prinsloo Maree, clerk; Robert Maree, clerk; and Sarel Gerhardus Rodgers, clerk.)

One of the men was driving. The car had stopped and could not be started. He told Masupha to push and promised him sixpence.

Masupha pushed the car and the engine started. He asked him for the 6d. He laughed and drove away. The car turned at a crossroads. He again asked for his money. The car stopped. One of the other men got out and slapped Masupha and said 'There!'

Masupha ran away. His assailant followed him, running. The other two men joined the chase. The three men caught him and put him in the car. The woman had remained sitting in the car.

Then they drove off, out of the little town. They stopped the car. The woman remained sitting in the car.

Then they took Masupha out of the car. One held his hands and one held his feet. The third stabbed Masupha in the private parts, injuring the scrotum and allowing one of the testicles to protrude, and hang out. He bled freely.

The men wanted to leave Masupha there, but the woman persuaded them to take him back to town. They left him on a pavement. His employer took him to hospital. (Ficksburg case 461/48.)

Masupha was not permanently injured. This case is small,

compared to others here recorded. Yet it contains the same elements as the worst.

It contains the element of injustice. The black man, because he counts for nothing, is cheated of the money he earned by co-operation.

It contains the element of sex.

It contains the element of recklessness, in that the assailants do not reck or care about the consequences of their acts to other human beings.

It contains the element of capricious tyranny: for daring to ask his all powerful 'master' for 6d, for daring to question the power and wisdom and goodness of his 'master', that 'master', aided by two friends, inflicts a dangerous wound.

It contains the element of frightfulness and '*Grausamkeit*': the wound is nicely placed where it will hurt, terrify, and injure most horribly.

The incident contains the element of tribal war. The three men attacked their tribal enemy. The woman sat witnessing this indecency, this unprovoked attack, and did not protest. For if she had protested as a woman might, she would have aligned herself with the 'enemies of her people'.

And it contains an element of international tension. Masupha's home was in Basutoland. He was assaulted in the Union of South Africa, simply because he was black. Thus does apartheid turn white men everywhere against black men everywhere and vice versa. Poisoning black-white relationships in the world as a whole, apartheid is not merely a domestic issue.

Both the Marais case and the Masupha case concerned young white men. For this fact the older generation bears a heavy responsibility. We have seen that the headmaster of the white school at Tzaneen taught his pupils to despise and loathe Africans by ritually burning a uniform jacket which an African had worn. Other members of the older generation also publicly incite violence and hatred against Africans. For example in 1962 a prominent Afrikaans-speaking member of the Uitenhage town council (Cape Province), speaking of disorders in the municipal market said of Africans who were unruly: 'We must get the full co-operation of Bantu Affairs, and the headman must be at the market more often. The sjambok must be put on them. It is the only thing that will help'. (*Sunday Tribune*, 25/3/62.) The sjambok, I remind readers, is a heavy rhinohide whip, thick and flexible, that can kill, and that is perhaps the most deadly whip in the world.

The guilt is not only the guilt of the older generation: it lies at the heart of modern South Africa, built into the constitution itself, which denies power, dignity, and status to all who are not white.

CHAPTER FIFTEEN

Conclusion

In this book I have recorded some of the evil fruits of the apartheid system.

Do not, please, imagine that this evil fruit is the exception, and that the tree of apartheid – save for these exceptions – may be good.

Even though whites do not normally torture their servants physically, most still treat them as sub-human. If a white person talks to another white person and turns to talk to a non-white person, his expression usually changes. A frown appears; a new note appears in the voice, a note of command. Children learn this voice and this look at the age of about four. Dogs sense their masters' hostility, and it is rare for a white person's dog not to be a racist – i.e. he fawns on whites and reserves his snarling for the non-whites.

The apartheid system does not merely produce a hell on earth for the non-whites; it distorts the personalities of all, of white as well as non-white.

It is a situation from which there is no orderly way out. Suggestions have been made that the country should be partitioned fairly. But Verwoerd himself has called such suggestions 'sheer foolishness'.

It is a situation which is endangering the good relations between white and non-white right round the world – and the greatest danger of the present day is that an irreconcilable schism will split the human race into two camps – the paler haves and the darker have-nots.

The South African situation is fundamentally unstable. No one any longer expects that a collapse can be avoided. The only question is: When?

CONCLUSION

Such stability as the apartheid state enjoys comes from the tacit shielding that it gets from certain countries in the West, notably the United Kingdom and France.

Britain and France continue to sell arms to the government of apartheid. And the farmers and police whose killings are reported in this book, probably killed with British arms and ammunition.

To continue this trade Britain is defying the Security Council resolution S5-386 of August 7, 1963 'solemnly calling on all states to cease forthwith the shipment of arms, ammunition, and of all types of military vehicles to South Africa'. Sixty-four other governments, including that of the United States, have complied. Britain's response to the appeal is to try to make a distinction between arms for internal security and arms for external defence.

The British government now says that it will not permit the export of arms that can be used 'to enforce apartheid'.

This distinction is quite meaningless. For instance, the British government is supplying Westland Wasp helicopters; yet no weapon is more useful for suppressing unrest. The truth of the matter is that all the energies of the South African government are directed towards 'enforcing apartheid'; all their arms including naval defence units, would be used for defending the totalitarian apartheid system against the anger of the world and of the majority of South Africans.

As reported in the South African government's own *Digest* of March 17, 1961, 'The minister of justice, Mr. F. C. Erasmus, and the minister of defence, Mr. J. J. Fouché, have announced that the South African Police and the Defence Force (army) will be reorganized on similar lines *so that they can provide a single fast striking force to crush any uprising regarded as a threat to the security of the state*'. (Author's emphasis.) 'In his Assembly speech, the minister of defence said "South Africa must pre-

137

pare for internal trouble in the same way as the major powers are continually preparing for war".'

How, in the light of this proudly aggressive acknowledgment by the South African government that all arms are for the suppression of uprisings and the maintenance of internal security, can the British government continue to make this distinction?

Thus, at the cost of its own integrity and to the peril of the international order maintained with so much difficulty by the United Nations, does the British government continue to arm and shield the government of apartheid.

As the Shangana-Tsonga people say: 'Loko mbyana yi ri ni rhambu enonwini, a yi vukuri', (when a dog has a bone in its mouth, it does not bark). Britain's 'bone' is £1,000 million invested in South Africa, plus a large favourable trade balance.

Perhaps the most disappointing feature of the British policy is that it inhibits the United States from a forward policy to solve the problem of apartheid.

The Americans are so powerful that if they were to call for a blockade against the supply of only one commodity, oil, to South Africa, the blockade would be imposed and the apartheid government would fall. The support of the Americans for the inherently much less effective western hemisphere sanctions against the Trujillo dictatorship in 1960 brought about its fall and the liberation of the Dominican Republic from an evil despotism.

The Americans are not yet ready to back an oil blockade against apartheid. And the principal reason for their unwillingness is the opposition of the British government.

One must respect the thoroughness with which the British government shields apartheid. They shield it from the Americans and from the independent African states. They shield it from its opponents in the neighbouring protectorates. They shield it at the United Nations. And they supply it with arms.

I love England. I owe my own education to this wonderful country. I am now as an exile privileged to enjoy its hospitality. For a century England has earned the gratitude of thousands of exiles. It is because I love and respect Britain that I am so disappointed at its present policy towards South Africa. I am sure that this policy stems from a lack of knowledge of what apartheid really is.

It is because of this lack of knowledge that I have written this book.

Take it, if you are British, to your friends, now that you have read it. Let them see what the true face of apartheid is. Let them know what is being shielded in their name.

For Product Safety Concerns and Information please contact our EU
representative GPSR@taylorandfrancis.com
Taylor & Francis Verlag GmbH, Kaufingerstraße 24, 80331 München, Germany

www.ingramcontent.com/pod-product-compliance
Lightning Source LLC
Chambersburg PA
CBHW050522280326
41932CB00014B/2421

9 7 8 1 0 3 2 3 3 3 6 3 2